MW01167398

CARLISLE WAY

by

Joan Schrager Cohen

To: Harriett,
— with much love,
Joan

PARKE PRESS

Norfolk, Virginia

Carlisle Way • Copyright © 2011 by Joan Schrager Cohen
All rights reserved.

All rights reserved, including the right to reproduce this work
in any form whatsoever without permission in writing from the
publisher, except for brief passages in connection with a review.

Book design: Marshall McClure

Published by
PARKE PRESS
Norfolk, Virginia

www.parkepress.com

ISBN 978-0-9843339-6-7

Library of Congress Control Number is available upon request

Printed in the United States of America

CONTENTS

Dedicated

to the DPs, the Jewish Displaced Persons
of Eastern Europe, post-Holocaust,
many of whom lost their lives wallowing
in the refugee camps.
To those who survived to tell
their stories, a light shines where
darkness dwelled.

Acknowledgments

To my cousin, David Rosenthal,
of blessed memory, who "lived" in
Auschwitz and Bergen-Belsen.
To Rabbi Michael Panitz,
Temple Israel, Norfolk, Virginia,
who guided me through narrating
the process of conversion,
the wedding ceremony and
the mourning of a loved one.

Carlisle Way

What we need as a couple is a more "human" love — one that will fulfill itself, infinitely considerate and gentle and good and clear in bending and releasing — that these two solitudes shall protect, touch, and greet one another.

Rainer Maria Rilke 1875–1926

CHAPTER ONE

Bess

*H*E WAS NOT AT ALL
what I had expected. As I swung the car into the driveway, I noticed he was standing by the garage alongside
John Reeves, the house painter. I brought the car to a stop,
letting the music from the tape deck linger a minute or so.
When I leaned over to shut it off, the man standing with
John turned toward me and through the open window
exclaimed, "Must be Gershwin!" His smile was broad and
warm. John made the introductions. Matthew Held was
his name. I marveled at the size of his hand as he offered
his grip – with a firmness that I suspected was most often
reserved for men. He was tall and lean – six feet at least.
The cadence of his words were not like John's – or any
of the other workmen who at one time or another found
their usefulness in the upkeep of Carlisle Way.

As we talked about ideas for the new porch and plans
to paint and repair the house, he looked squarely at me.
His gaze was direct. Brown eyes with specks of yellow. His
beard was scrubbed clean and neatly trimmed. His longish
hair, which he wore like a mantle, seemed shorter on one
side, allowing the visibility of a small earring. Although his

9

hair was turning grey, one could see where blond and fair-haired-brown still mingled.

As we talked, I envisioned Matthew Held as a Confederate general. He could have gracefully carried off the grey uniform of a Confederate officer and its accompanying regalia, complete with dangling sword. His bearing and stature called for some type of splendor! So straight and erect for a tall man, I remember thinking on that day. For someone his size and age (late forties or early fifties) there were no visible signs of stooping or hunching over. Life's configurations and convoluted ironies – its countless inequities – had not yet cowed Matthew Held!

I was intrigued with Matthew from the beginning. I observed every nuance and detail of him from the spread of his shoulders to the way his clothes hung loosely on his lanky frame and how he tilted his head back to puff on a cigarette.

It was in the heat of summer when we first met. His cut-off jeans allowed me to see his muscled, lean legs. He was slim and lithe of body, and I sensed his palate was easily satisfied with foods of the earth.

John explained that Matthew would be doing most of the painting and repairing of Carlisle Way. He, John, had to be on another job most of the time. I recall feeling secretly glad at that.

Thinking back to when I became aware of the stirrings that Matthew caused in my mind and body, I realized it was nothing he did or said. It was simply his presence. Whenever he spoke or moved or exerted any effort, it was done with deliberate ease. He seemed embraced by the energy of wind and sun.

David had always said that my face was an open book and that I could never hide my true feelings. I wondered if Matthew noticed the color rising in my cheeks whenever he stood near. His stare was too direct, not sufficiently vacant. Did he take note, too, of the goose flesh as it appeared on my forearm when his hand accidentally brushed by me?

Matthew exuded strength and gentleness all at the same time. I noticed the way he spoke to the neighborhood children, our housekeeper, or the postman. If it was servitude, it was an elegant servitude. When the grandchildren came to visit, he drew them out in conversation with meaningful questions and answers.

Sometimes he engaged Amy and Alex in play, like the day I found the three of them blowing bubbles. "No, no, Matthew," Amy exclaimed. "Not like that! You'll swallow the stuff!" How distinctly I can see it all now. The sun shone through the clouds, not letting the cumulus mountain take it over completely. There, sitting on the steps of the side porch, was Matthew Held, earnestly listening to a rather impatient five-year-old female who was determined to teach him the art of blowing bubbles! I thought it so strange when Matthew later claimed he had not been allowed such frivolities as a child.

And then there was the day I was making fresh flower arrangements for the sitting room when I heard Matthew's laughter. Soon, Amy's giggle was evident, a giggle that always reminded me of the hummingbird, who, when sated by our special feeder hung near the back porch, would set off the chimes in a delicate, lyrical way. As I looked from the window, trying not to let my spying become known, I saw Amy climbing on Matthew's back as he was desperately trying to draw lines in chalk for her and her friends! On the pretense of taking out the stagnant water and the flowers now devoid of life, I stood only a few feet away from them. Matthew sensed I was there, as he always did, and looked up at me in his rather bemused way. "Can you believe this? If I draw hopscotch lines for these gals, they've promised to teach me how to play!" His shy grin and easy manner endeared him to the children. They often asked, "Is Matthew coming today, Nana?"

Matthew was circumspect about taking up my time or lingering too long in the kitchen. His concern for propriety was evident. He showed an interest in our progeny and seemed to take delight in our family photos, which were framed like a "rogues' gallery" down the long hallway visible from the kitchen.

Matthew had a keen eye. He took in every aspect of wherever he happened to be. When he came inside for a cold drink or to use the bathroom, he might comment about some painting or artifact, or an arrangement I had made for one of the tables. Nothing missed his discerning eye. Matthew, I came to find out, was an artist who worked in several mediums. Clay, acrylic, watercolor and ceramics were but a few.

Occasionally Matthew worked alongside me. He had an ear for listening to a woman, I thought back then. I found, too, that Matthew Held valued his privacy, as I did mine. We talked about the strength one finds in solitude and the serenity of repose that comes of it. He seemed to be unencumbered by life's possessions or its ordinary societal rituals. Matthew Held had a depth of understanding that I had not seen in a man in my rather brief acquaintances with men. With the exception of my dearest friend, Dr. Stephen Sohlberg, and David, whom I had met in college, I knew little of how men thought and felt.

Once when we were working in the garden, planting pots of impatiens and geraniums, I sensed his need to talk. "How did you come to live in Nansemond County,

Matthew?" I asked.

He answered easily. "I was born and raised not too far from here – along the Eastern Shore – a smallish town – a fishing village – where my maternal grandparents had passed down some good farmland. It's near Accomac. You know the area?"

"Oh, yes. We used to rent, in Wachapreague, David and I, a cottage near there in the summers when the children were at camp. Just lie about, read books. I'd do a little writing – no TV or telephones. It was quite peaceful. Has it changed much – I mean – have you had occasion to go back?"

"I've gone back a few times, but each time I do I become saddened. There are hardly any young folks anymore – or even people my age. They've gone off to the big cities. Many farms were bought out by chicken packers. It's just not the same quaint place I remember growing up – it seems to lack the comfort of people looking out for each other."

"When did you leave there, Matt?"

"I earned a degree in fine arts at The University. Got my first job in New York. I was a restless son-of-a-gun, though! Began zigzagging between the east and west coasts – going from window and floor display manager at some of the more well-known department stores – like Gimbels and Macy's – to The May Company, and Gump's out west. Soon that bored me, too. So I became a scenic designer for small opera houses and repertory theaters around the country. During the last recession, I got caught in the downsizing.

"But that all coincided with what I term big-city-burnout," declared Matthew. "I was ready to fold the tent anyway. I longed for the smell of fresh air – to get my hands back into the earth – to see things grow again. I wanted to concentrate on my art, too. And then, both my parents are in their eighties. I'm an only child, so it just seemed the right thing to do – to move back while I still have some time with them. Being a bachelor all these years and being frugal, I saved up a considerable nest egg – bought myself a house."

He talked about how well his new landscaping business was doing and that some of his art work had recently been accepted in nearby art shows and museums. Perhaps reading my mind, Matthew assured me that doing household repairs and yard work were not "beneath him."

Each morning when Matthew arrived, I observed him from the kitchen window. He would tie a scarf around his forehead to catch the perspiration. I watched intently as the sun glistened off the sweat of his body. I liked to see him hose himself off, dutifully removing and folding his shirt beforehand.

When the temperature reached nearly one-hundred, I went to find an old straw hat of David's and asked Matthew if he cared to wear it. He turned the hat over and over in his hands, softening its edges. "How thoughtful," he said, with that warm, shy grin of his. Painstakingly he donned the hat at a jaunty, tilted angle, tucking his long hair underneath its brim.

DAVID'S HAT. David. Two years since he'd been gone. I had loved my husband David, in my own fashion, as I believe he had loved me. But he had always been limited in his expression of love or in his emotional venting – keeping things close to the vest – his feelings in lockstep. He came from a cold, undemonstrative family – a family of "quiet" men. David was a tense and driven man – very involved in his practice – singular of purpose, be it his work, or golfing, or investing in the stock market!

David's bouts of melancholy came more often after the death of his younger sister. I found it more difficult with each passing year to purge him of this affliction. It exhausted my energies. And then came the women and the drinking. Worse, I think now, were the walled silences – his remote and reclusive behavior.

In the last ten years or so, before David's death, I would sometimes succumb to despair when I ultimately faced up to the ills of our marriage. But I was not one to dwell on that which was impossible to change. While David's despondency, exacerbated by his drinking, saddened me and kept distance between us, I think that on balance, we had had love and passion and a good life for most of the years we lived together.

I had not been apprised of David's manic depression, more than likely inherited from his mother, when we first met. I don't think even David understood why he found himself in such uneven emotional states so frequently until he, much later in life, unearthed his family history. Even armed with his medical training, he seemed unable to give up alcohol, knowing full well its implications when combined with manic depression.

Strange how I felt more attached to David in his death than when he was here on this earth. I remember reading once, perhaps at a funeral service, "We see them now with the eye of memory; their faults forgiven, their virtues grown large. Goodness lives where weakness fades." But even in the latter years of our marriage we had drawn comfort from one another and had settled into a rhythmic pattern of living. We had sustained each other during moments of crises. We had built a web together – enduring bonds.

Remarkably, I found myself opening up to Matthew in a way that David had never permitted me to do. But I did not know what to make of this attraction to Matthew. I was perplexed and confused. There were so many questions I posed to myself.

Was there a woman in Matthew's life? In spite of a healthy diet and daily exercise, my body could not compete with that of a younger woman. Gravity will have its way! Was he promiscuous? I must tread lightly, I kept thinking. Perhaps, I thought, at my age, one's judgment was flawed as to attention derived from someone of the opposite sex. Could I – would I – intrude upon his life?

I wondered what he did, where he went, whom he spent time with when he was absent from Carlisle Way. Was I reaching out to Matthew Held as a way of confronting my own impending mortality? Or was I simply trying to stave off old age and loneliness?

They say fantasies arise out of anxiety. But what was I anxious about? I could not think of a single thing. Did only the gods know of the reason for this vision – for this kind of longing? If I am restless at all, I thought, it is a restlessness of the spirit, not the body. But can they be separated? I was no longer sure of anything.

On the few dates with widowers and divorced men that my friends had arranged for me, I did not feel I was betraying David's memory or tarnishing the life we shared. But now, this compelling need for Matthew Held had brought on pangs of guilt. Perhaps it was so because I found myself physically attracted to Matthew. Worrisome images crept into my mind – seeing the earring – wondering about Matthew's sexuality. Like many of my generation, I was probably a prisoner of preconceived notions concerning gay or effeminate men – or what I thought gay or effeminate men looked like or acted! But what if he were in fact gay or bisexual? If either were true, what then would I make of my feelings toward him?

How would I handle this? Had providence sent Matthew Held to me at this juncture of my life? My state of being brought to mind William Faulkner's words, "a human heart in conflict with itself."

Whenever Matthew took a break or had lunch, he propped himself up against one of the large magnolia trees on the far side of the house. Slowly pulling out his pocket radio, he would search for a classical station to his liking. With closed eyes, he often ate lunch tapping his fingers along the metal lunchbox, keeping time to the music. All of these pictures of him act as imprimaturs upon my mind, so well am I reminded of his look – his smile – seeing him at work or in thought.

Even though David's and my son had grown and married, I had left the basketball hoop up and the backboard intact. The neighborhood children knew they were welcome. Alex, our grandson, noticed that Matthew was left-handed, just like he was. "Matt," he asked, "are you good at a left-handed hook shot?"

"Sure am, Alex, pass the ball over here and we'll have a go at it."

Alex revealed to me later that day Matthew's story of how his father had smacked his hands, even as an infant, to change him to a rightie. "Didn't take," was Matthew's comment to Alex. "I resisted him all the way!" But Matthew confided in Alex that he and his Dad, while estranged for many years, had since become friends and were "working things out. "

One day, in the heat of that summer, when Matthew and I were dancing to a song whose words we couldn't hear, but whose melody coursed through us, I invited him into the kitchen to join Amy and me for lunch. I likened it to having a "cooling-off spell." He willingly obliged.

While we were seated and I was pouring lemonade,

Amy stared hard at Matthew as only a five-year-old can. "Why do you wear that earring, Matthew? Earrings are for ladies!"

I, too, had looked skeptically at that earring. The question of "why?" had been on the tip of my tongue for months. Yet I could not be so forward as to ask. But wonder I had. And I think Matthew knew that I had glanced sidelong at it. As I was about to admonish Amy for her intrusion into Matthew's private world, he answered her. "Well now, Amy – let's see – well, this is the '90s and many people, both men and women alike, wear earrings, especially if they are craftspersons." While explaining to Amy what a craftsperson was, Matthew seemed to be searching my face for the credulity of his reply and my reaction. Was he wondering if I thought him gay? While I harbored no prejudice against gays, I wanted so much for Matthew to be straight.

After Amy had gone home, Matthew offered to help me clear the table. As we approached the sink, our arms collided. I did not draw away from him, nor did he move his arm from touching mine. Rather I felt him lean into me, or was this self-deception – the lie or the illusion created by a vulnerable woman?

Within a year of knowing Matthew Held, I was not only physically fascinated with him, but also emotionally and spiritually attracted. This much I knew: If his hand touched mine when he handed me something or I to him, I would feel almost faint. His eyes were so intently upon me whenever we talked that I sometimes wondered how I managed to carry on a conversation.

Matthew took in what I wore, and whatever I was doing. He noticed if I was rested or tired, but not in any lustful or leering way. There were no furtive glances; nothing wanton in his look. This was a man of discretion, of that I was sure.

How I recall the day I decided to wear a long, flowy skirt and lace-up sandals, instead of my usual tailored garb! As I walked toward the car, Matthew just stopped what he was doing. He stood there, leaning on his rake. He made a sweeping bow and uttered, "Bewitching, Madame Cantin, simply bewitching! A sight for sore eyes, you are," using a cockney accent which he often did in jest.

Thoughts of Matthew Held ruminated through my mind, wherever I was, whatever I was doing. Gradually I realized I would not be able to quell my desire for him, to suppress my feelings. Was all of this a seduction of sorts – an inner longing for intimacy – a longing apparently ignored 'til now? It was there, no matter how hard I denied its existence. It was there – just below the surface of the skin.

CHAPTER TWO

Matthew

*A*S WE DROVE
'cross town toward Carlisle Way, John Reeves filled me in on the Cantins. Seems as though John's father had done most of the painting and repairing when the Cantins bought the place about twenty-five years ago.

"I figure she must have been about thirty-three or so back then," John said. "I used to go along with Dad on Saturdays or after school, as his helper. You know, hand him things and all. I must have been about eight or nine. Man, she was a beauty – and stacked! I mean, built! Dad says she's always been a real lady – not afraid to get her hands dirty, either. The husband, he was a big-time M.D. Nice sort, but wasn't around much. Had a real busy practice; played a lot of golf. You know the type! David Cantin died about two years ago. Knocked the starch out of her!"

My curiosity led me to question John as to why she kept the big house. "Beats me, Matt. Dad and I figure it's because she's rooted in the earth of Carlisle Way. Loves to garden. No way I could picture Bess Cantin in some condo or an apartment."

I was thinking to myself, yet an audible voice was heard to say, "It's her refuge, I suppose." John was shifting gears in the pickup and had only half heard me. And so I repeated: "She takes refuge from Carlisle Way." John, keeping ever-vigilant on the curving road, nodded his head in agreement.

"There she is!" John pointed with a degree of pride. "There's Carlisle Way!"

I was struck not only by the size of the house, but by its linear quality. It took up practically the entire street called Carlisle Way. It was an old home, maybe fifty or sixty years old, but well kept. Although it was common in this part of the South to find two-story homes with columns, this one was unusual. The roof was made of Spanish tile, clay in color; the exterior walls of the façade were off-white clapboard. The gables and shutters, of which there were many, were painted in the green of moss and fern. Around the wrought iron gates, shrubs of pink and white winter camellias were symmetrically poised with oleander. Holly and boxwood adorned the far side walls and they, too, appeared geometrically arranged. Surrounding on all of its other sides were huge magnolia trees. Yet it was the towering oaks and elms that lent a majesty to Carlisle Way.

I thought: a weathered, but stately home – still reveling in its southern gentility with an ageless grace. From what John told me, the upkeep of Carlisle Way had been, in his words, a "mission" of Bess Cantin's. She has done it well, I recall thinking.

John and I were in the midst of a conversation when Bess Cantin pulled into the driveway. I could hear the strains of a Gershwin melody coming from the car.

As she swung her legs out of the car and walked toward us, I was caught off-guard by her vigorous, athletic stride that defied her age. According to John's calculations, Bess was in her mid- to late fifties. Yet there was a certain verve to the woman that I was immediately attracted to.

She was lovely. My eyes saw what once was, and what still remained. As I approached the car, with John beside me making the introductions, she extended her hand and did not shirk from my hearty handshake.

One needs the soul of a poet, I suppose, to describe her hair as she bent down in that late afternoon sunlight as we studied plans for rebuilding the porch. The golds and russets of autumn with subtle strands of silver here and there. Yes, I said to myself, she is autumn. Her greenish-grey eyes looked deep inside you – and crinkled when she talked. Even when Bess Cantin was serious about something, a smile would somehow cast itself across her face. As I observed her more closely, I discovered the lines around the eyes and mouth; the "living" lines, I like to call them – lines associated with hours of lost sleep, worrying over children and grandchildren or, perhaps, trying to work things out with a husband.

"David would have asked – 'is this necessary?'," Bess surmised out loud, joking with John and me about how her late husband would have been grumpy about spending any further money on the gardens or the house. "I think David thought things at Carlisle Way would somehow just stand still – simply take care of themselves," she said, with a faraway look in her eyes. Almost as an afterthought, she added, "I suspect David had enough 'human disrepair' to contend with in his practice to worry over Carlisle Way."

Later, when John and I were driving home, he told me about the tensions and conflicts in this upper-middle class milieu, underlying the marriage of Bess and David Cantin. And that David's medical practice – the attempt to save lives – had caused him great anguish when he realized his own inadequacy and vulnerability.

I thought for the first time how grappling with death on a daily basis would exact a heavy toll on a relationship – especially a marriage.

JOHN REEVES' father was one of David Cantin's heart patients and knew the Cantin family well. "Laid actual hands on my Dad, David did," John confided, "open heart surgery. Saved my Dad's life! My Dad says the way Dr. Cantin dealt with the stress of his work was through escape. He played hard, drank hard, and there was talk a while back about some skirt chasing!"

As the days of summer wore on, I came to be at Carlisle Way several days a week, doing the painting and repairs practically by myself, with John helping out occasionally. I watched Bess come and go. She seemed a purposeful woman, bent on whatever task was at hand. She was of a pleasant disposition. I liked to listen to the banter between her and her housekeeper, Maggie, or whoever was in the house with her. Her voice had a timbre – a lilt – that at times beguiled me – unsettled me. When she would leave messages on my answering machine, I often played them back, searching for that enigmatic quality. Her voice, while not suggestive or sensual, had an earthy tone and a slight twinge of a drawl, giving off a distant impression of girlishness mixed with womanly know-how.

When she was working in one of the gardens, her clothes were of a Hepburnish era: khaki pants, a starched and tailored white shirt rolled to the elbow, open sandals and a floppy straw to protect her fairness. "If I'm not careful, Matthew," she told me, "I turn into one big freckle by summer's end!"

One day, Bess drove up with her little granddaughter, Amy, who ran to me, pouting. "Matthew, Matthew, do you think Nana is ugly? The lady at the beauty parlor cut her hair too short and now Nana thinks she's ugly!" Amy's query brought me up short. Bess Cantin, ugly? Never! All I could think to say was, "No, Amy, your Nana is *not* ugly. She looks *just* fine!" Bess flashed an appreciative glance in my direction. "I'm like the biblical Samson, who loses his strength when his hair is shorn," she retorted.

But her true strength was derived from Carlisle Way and when she was absent from it, as she explained to me months later, she pined, the way a parent misses a child, or a lover his love. She talked about her love of "place" – of Carlisle Way – with particular words of reverence. It was not merely a love of place for Bess, as I saw it, but an ode to a time when things had meaning – and she wanted to preserve what was good so it would live on.

"You'd have made an impressive Heathcliff," she had called out to me the day I stood atop the roof of Carlisle Way, cleaning its gutters and valleys. Her words – her way of expressing herself – often had a way of disarming me.

Lately, I had begun to feel a gnawing sensation that something had gone awry in the course I had charted for myself. Through the years I had kept my own good counsel, enjoying the soul's replenishment through my hours of solitude. Painting, sculpting, my fondness for gardening had been sources of fulfillment in a well-ordered regimen. I was not hindered by a desire for material worth, nor did I much care about society's demands. There had not been loneliness, until now.

As a child, I had contracted a severe case of encephalitis, and the residue of this affliction had been impotency. Yet, I had been no stranger to women – intelligent, kindhearted and attractive women. They had found me virile in spite of the impotency. Perhaps, because of this "defect" in me, I learned how to listen to a woman and to develop a sensitivity to her needs.

I THINK I fell in love with Bess Cantin the first day we met. With each succeeding visit to Carlisle Way, I became convinced that she was a woman I had to know. I cannot deny that I wished to make love to her in my own way. Yet I knew from the start that I was drawn to her in ways more powerful than merely the physical. It was the cerebral about her that bedeviled me!

What defined her for me? She was a woman completely herself; no mask, no armor. There was a studied seriousness about Bess Cantin embedded in her responses. I was often moved by her show of compassion and commitment to whatever she believed in.

In my mind's eye, she was still a beautiful woman. She had a spirit – a vitality – a zest for life. I thought of Bess as a paradox, an incongruity. There was a modern-day feminism there, yet it was coupled with old-fashioned ways. Her sensibilities moved me, of that I was sure. She was inside my head, whether I was near her or not.

During those warm summer months, when I would be outside painting, Bess let the house at Carlisle Way be cooled by its many ceiling fans. The windows remained open till late afternoon. Thus, I could hear her at the Steinway. She often played when alone. The strains of a Liszt piano concerto, or a Chopin polonaise would move me in such a way that I had to pause in my work. But it was when she played "Sweet Remembrances" from Mendelssohn's "Songs Without Words" that she brought tears to my eyes. Although Bess was far from a concert pianist, she played with a poignancy that spoke of her sensitive nature. Her deepest emotion, be it joy or sadness, was most often expressed through music, either in the selection she chose to listen to on the stereo or the pieces she so passionately embraced on the piano. Her own favorite, I came to discover, was the fourth movement of Beethoven's Ninth Symphony, "The Ode To Joy."

While Bess derived satisfaction and a certain spirituality from within the walls of herself and of Carlisle Way, there were other dimensions to this woman.

Although she admitted her books had not been financially successful, Bess Cantin had been a writer of children's books for many years.

She jealously guarded her grandchildren and took delight in spending time with them. To watch her – the easy give-and-take in their movements and conversation – made her even more desirable to me. I found sensuality in her touch of Amy and Alex and in the way she tenderly spoke to them.

Bess instinctively anticipated what I was thinking or about to say, or what I needed. I would look up and she would be standing there with a pitcher of ice water or a sandwich – or a straw hat (which belonged to David) to shield me from the hot sun. One day she surprised me with a birthday dinner and cake all wrapped in foil for me to carry home. Now and then she called to talk about the unusual bloom of a flower we had planted or how much she liked what I had done in one of the gardens. I had never known anyone as intuitive as Bess Cantin. Yet this intuition was managed with great subtlety.

During the winter months, when outdoor landscaping was almost nonexistent, Bess asked me if I minded doing some indoor tasks – like helping her clean the attic or relining the pantry shelves. Maggie, her housekeeper, was getting on in years. I would have done it for free, to be near her, but I knew this would not set well with Bess.

We were in the attic, rummaging through old boxes of frames and scrapbooks, when she saw me staring at a photo of David with someone younger than he, but who closely resembled him. Bess explained that it was Clara Lee, David's younger sister and only sibling, who had died of Lou Gehrig's disease in her forties. "David's bouts of melancholia came more often after Clara Lee's passing," she observed. "David never really got over it."

Along the corridor, which lay between the kitchen and family room where Bess and I were taking some pictures down and putting others up, she brought up the subject of David and the kind of a man he was – things he did and said – his foibles and virtues. I had the impression that David loomed larger in Bess's memory than in his actual living. I had read somewhere about the myth we create about our loved ones – a longing for what wasn't there – a wish that he or she could have been other than what actually was.

By this time, I would have given almost anything to exorcise myself from this obsession with Bess. The purist in me made me wonder if this love, left unrequited, might have much to be said for it. But Bess Cantin had evoked in me a need for a part of life that had, thus far, eluded me.

CHAPTER THREE

Matthew and Bess

THE DAWN HADN'T come upon us yet that morning when I arose. It was my day to be at Carlisle Way and as always, when I was going to see Bess, I was possessed of an eager anticipation. Something was happening between us. I felt it in my marrow – saw it in her face – heard it embedded in her responses.

Amid the sounds of nature that come along in the half-light of morning, I found the shirt that pleased her, the blue-and-beige plaid, and began to iron it. It was still too early to leave for Carlisle Way.

As the iron glided slowly across the fabric, I saw before me an incident which had heartened me. It had occurred only a week ago when we were adjusting the stakes for the tomato plants – with both of us "on bended knee," as Bess so aptly phrased the posture we find ourselves in when we garden.

The hot sun bore down on us. As we worked side by side, I noticed the sweat on the nape of Bess's slender neck, like early morning dew. Impulsively, I reached out with my kerchief. I was about to wipe away the beads of perspiration from her neck as they trickled down her back, when she turned to me and smiled. Softly, she said, "It's all right, Matthew, I'll do it." And then she gently reached up and stroked my cheek with the kerchief before wiping herself off. I saw the fluster; the trembling hands.

Today, maybe tomorrow, soon — I remember thinking that day — I would have to confront Bess with the fact of my impotency. Would she spurn me? Others had. Would she turn away from me because I was only half a man? I would make known my feelings for her, no matter that it might mean leaving Carlisle Way and never seeing Bess again.

IT HAPPENED that day, as I somehow knew it would.

The unmistakable laughter of Bess; the shrieks and squeals of little Amy — pierced me — brought me up short from what I was doing. When I came 'round to the back of the house where they were playing, I found myself motionless — transfixed.

As Bess tended to Amy's pale skin, smoothing suntan oil lovingly upon the child's shoulders and back, I became awash in my desire for Bess to touch me — to caress me — the way in which she did Amy.

Bess felt my eyes upon her; could read my thoughts. I was convinced this was so. After Amy left, Bess came outside and stood close behind me as I knelt on the ground, finishing up the weeding. Even before she touched me lightly on the shoulder, I knew by the warm smell of her that she was there. I leaned back against her legs, so aware of her presence. Slowly I stood and turned. I slipped my arm around her waist; pulled her gently to me. Bess lay her head on my chest. I kissed the top of it, I being a good foot or more taller than she. We stood like that for a long time, holding tightly to one another, breathing in the moment of revelation. Words were not spoken then, nor were they needed.

EVENTUALLY they talked for a very long time. She needed to know about his life, even after she had heard it all before. He told her stories of his youth, of his yearnings, of his misbegotten dreams and of his unhappiness as a child. His stern, military father had been harsh with him.

Matthew had not been allowed the ordinary playfulness of a little boy. There were the chores, the lists posted on the wall. Only gold stars or blue, good or bad, no in-between. As a small child, Matthew was often left alone with his mother as his father was flying with the Strategic Air Command in combat missions over Korea. He and his mother lived in Tokyo at the time. Matthew remembered the fear in which he held his father. When Captain Held came home for R&R, Matthew would hide behind the couch. His father's voice frightened him. "He drank heavily and was often verbally abusive to my mother," recalled Matthew. "You're coddling that boy! I know he sleeps in your bed when I'm not here!" Douglas Held would rant and rave.

As Matthew related all of this to Bess, she began to feel he was preparing her for the fact that he was gay. There was the earring, the harshness and lack of intimacy with his father. She knew it was coming. But, she said to herself, "I don't care, even if he is gay. I love this man. I want him in my life."

As Matthew reached out to her, Bess laid her head upon his lap and began to quietly sob. He tilted her head gently upward, kissing her tears – holding her at a distance. Each of them searched the other's eyes – he, to tell the truth about himself, she, to implore him that whatever it was, it would not matter. She loved him. Her eyes told him that. She gave him the courage to go on.

"I'm impotent, Bess, from a childhood bout of encephalitis," he uttered. "It's irreversible."

"Oh, my love – when, how?"

"I was ten years old. It was while we were living in Tokyo. I contracted a serious case of encephalitis. They didn't think I was going to make it. Maybe, if we had been living in the States, with better medical treatment, the right drugs, the residue of the disease would not have been what it was. I don't know. None of the doctors would attest to that."

While Matthew explained to Bess that he could not make love to her in the conventional way, the way a man wants to, it was as if Bess had not heard a word he said. She did not answer him. Instead, she brought his hands to her mouth, kissing each long and graceful finger. With a wry and knowing smile, she unbuttoned her white, pristine shirt. She slowly guided Matthew's hands along the contours of her breasts and across the flesh of her abdomen, then downward over the jutting edges of her womanly hips and finally deep within her. She came to him over and over. It was like nothing she had ever known.

Later, as they talked, they held each other closely, kissing and touching one another. Bess was thinking, yes, this is good – it's enough for me. I feel complete within the circle of his arms, to receive his touch, to feel his mouth upon mine.

Matthew's beautiful hands, those long tapering fingers with artistic grace, caressed her, touched her everywhere, awakened every part of her being, until she cried out his name, begging him to never leave her. And there were tears in the corners of his eyes. Bess would never forget them.

As they stood there in Bess's studio, saying goodbye for the day, holding each other, it was as if a layer of gossamer had dissolved upon them. They were engulfed within the framework of each other's bodies. They could see nothing to either side of them, only each other. They would be unable to know or to say, if questioned, where they were standing in that room. They could only see and feel each other and how they were encompassed by the weight of their bodies pressed together.

CHAPTER FOUR

Bess

"*T*HE FEATURES OF your face are indelibly drawn in my mind. If I were blind, I could draw them," Matthew spoke, closing his eyes. He gently allowed his fingers to graze lightly upon Bess' forehead. He barely touched the small, upward curve of her nose – then her lips. Lovingly he cupped her face in his hands.

"Why the earring, Matthew?"

"My craft, simply that."

"I wondered."

"I know. I could sense it. The way you stared at it; at me."

"Well, it wasn't just the earring. Your sensitivity and all. Oh, how stereotypical of me! Because of your capacity for so many forms of art, I assumed, I ...."

"I know, I know, Bess. I understand."

"Hold me, darling, hold me. What must it have been like for you, with your beautiful face, and body, how did you.... There must have been other women – younger, lovely women. How jealous I am of them all!"

"I've actually had very few women in my life,

Bess. Some were initially attracted to me, but when they discovered the impotency, they couldn't handle it. They wanted traditional lovemaking."

"Was there ever anyone you came to love and wanted to marry?"

"Yes. But she wanted children, so we eventually parted.

"And you, my Bess. Was there ever another man in your life besides David? A woman like you, so giving, so full of love! There must have been others – especially with David such a closed man."

She paused, then answered. "It happened just once, Matt, only once. I was taking a college course in bioethics. This was after the children were grown and in college – perhaps they had even graduated by then. I'm not sure of the actual time frame. I had been a pre-law student in the years before my marriage to David and had always been interested in the ethical dilemmas presented by these two fields. A close friend of ours, David's and mine, Stephen Sohlberg, an internist, had left his medical practice and gone back to school to study psychiatry. He was teaching this course through his association with the medical school. A local attorney taught the legal half.

"Stephen was an interesting man – *is*, I should say. I have always been impressed by his intellect. The four of us – he and his wife, Sylvia and David and I – had been good friends in college and medical school. Although a full professor at the medical school, Stephen retained a small private practice in psychiatry. I had never sought therapy, feeling these things to be a private matter – no one else's concern – just the natural crises of life one has to attend to. But I came to a juncture where I needed a therapist."

Bess went on, haltingly. "It was about nine or ten years ago. Our marriage had reached a low ebb. David couldn't bring himself to admit he had a drinking problem or that he was deeply depressed. The fact of his alcoholism remained unknown to even his closest colleagues, so secretive was he, so clever in his methods of camouflage. But it had become nearly intolerable to me, the way in which he chose to handle this disparity at home. David had begun drinking more heavily after his sister's death, the liquor priming the rage within. His bouts of melancholia came more often. I pleaded with him to seek professional help. He refused. So I went to Stephen to learn how to survive and to cope with David. At least, in the beginning, that was my motivation."

"What was there about Stephen that attracted you? I assume this is the man you are about to tell me you had an affair with," Matthew inquired, with what Bess detected as a twinge of jealousy.

"Well, he is alternately thoughtful and raucous; an intellectual with great sensitivity. Our friendship grew, ripening into admiration, then respect and soon something akin to love," declared Bess, for the moment ignoring Matt's comment about "an affair."

"I don't know exactly, Matthew, what attracted me to this man. Perhaps it was seeing Stephen lecturing to his students or talking one-on-one with one of them. Something about seeing him at his craft – it was like an aphrodisiac!

"There has always been an aura of mysticism about Stephen – a kind of lyric poetry. When I first heard him lecture, what he evoked in me was quite strange and wonderful – although in some way disquieting. I felt enveloped by a warm light, a glow, and I can still remember feeling a sense of contentment, as if finding something I had long been searching for.

"He had – I mean, he has – this incredible speaking

voice," Bess went on. "The sound of it, when I first sat in on his lectures, would put me in a kind of hypnotic state. Yes, I suppose, of all that I can recall or remember about him and how I went from friendship to love with this man, what lingers in my mind most profoundly is that velvet and melodic voice – soft, deep lingering tones, well modulated, that somehow calmed me and from which I drew comfort. And there is the shape of his mouth. His lips are like those of a woman – heart-shaped and full, often set in a semi-smile of beneficence; cherub-like."

"I suppose he was, I mean, is, terribly good-looking," Matthew ventured.

"No, Matt, honestly, he is far from being physically attractive. He's short and rather portly; wears thick glasses and is going bald – has been for years. There, does that make you feel better?" Bess quipped, reaching out to Matthew, kissing him hard on the mouth.

"Matt, if you only understood what it was like for me! I feared that I would become what David had become – a despondent and angry person. I had thought of leaving several times, but by this point in time, it was too late. David was sick and needed me. I felt bereft and betrayed by life. I needed someone to guide me through this impasse. To Stephen, it is a sin to succumb to dismay. He would not let me fall to common ways. I was wandering in the wilderness and he brought me through it safely," and Bess began crying softly.

"Oh, Bess. I'm just jealous of anyone who was that close to you – who meant that much to you. But I do understand," Matthew said as he reached out to hold her.

"It didn't take much to stoke David's simmering anger," Bess went on. "His rancor would erupt in a rage at the slightest provocation. He had lost his parents at a young age and then his sister. Some of his heart patients could not be saved, some of whom were lifelong friends. David had always been possessed of a certain hubris and carried himself in a stoic manner. He hid his drinking and his temper quite well. I was probably the only one who really knew."

"How did you make known your love for one another – you and Stephen?" Matt asked.

"Stephen's abiding gentleness, which was reflected in his voice and manner – in the words he chose – allowed me inside. I began sharing ideas with him on medical/legal topics. I clipped articles that I thought he'd be interested in and would drop them off in his message box at the university. I consumed all his extra reading assignments as if awakening from a deep slumber. After class I often found myself standing by his desk. He'd pull out a chair for me, and we would talk and talk. Besides his psychiatric background, Stephen is also a deeply religious man. He often counseled me on how to draw upon the ideology of Judaism for strength during my ordeal. He is well-versed in the Talmud and Torah, the pillars of Jewish learning."

"I didn't realize you were Jewish!"

"Is that a problem?"

"Oh my God, no, Bess. I just never gave it a thought."

"Didn't you notice the religious symbols in the house? The mezuzzahs on the doors, the Israeli clock, the pictures of the children at their Bar and Bat Mitzvahs?"

"Bess, I never paid them any mind! I guess I was too engrossed in just looking at you, darling." Matthew reached for Bess' hand and drew her into his lap.

Bess continued, "Initially I had trepidation about telling Stephen about my attraction to him. But on the phone, after he had been away, I mentioned I wanted to come and see him. He said, 'Your voice is a welcome sound.' And then, just before hanging up the phone that day, he said, 'I look forward all *too* much to your visits, Bess. We need to talk about this when you come.'

"On the occasion of my next therapy session, he at first didn't bring up the subject of what was happening between us. But when I stood to leave, he suddenly took hold of my hands, and with a touchingly sweet look, uttered, 'You give me so much, Bess.' I suppose it was those six words that began our 'affinity of the soul' relationship. Stephen would say things like, 'I delight in your presence' or 'I bask in your warmth.' 'Come sit beside me, Bess', he would often say, beckoning me with his eyes. Placing my hand in his, I'd curl up beside him, with my feet tucked under me, resting my head on his shoulder as he stroked my hair."

"That's it? That's all?" Matthew asked in astonishment.

"Yes, Matt. Stephen's principles never allowed him to even think of going further. In all honesty, I was not that noble of heart. I'm sure had he relented, we would have had a liaison."

Matt didn't say a word. He let go of Bess and reached for a cigarette.

"Oh, Matt, all of this is making you uncomfortable! But you wanted to know everything and I'm telling you all of it! We never ever made love – never consummated our relationship – at least not in the way you're thinking. We made love with our eyes, with our voices – our words. And Stephen guided me – shepherded me through the terrible odyssey of David's illness and his eventual death.

"I am being perfectly honest. I yearned for Stephen with such a passion and longing, so starved was I for emotional intimacy! While David and I always had – except at the end – sexual compatibility, David was not a man that was inner-reflective, nor did he like to talk very much about feelings. It was only upon knowing Stephen that I discovered what I had been missing all of my married life. David and I, although in love for much of our married life, never shared this kind of 'spiritual affinity.' When I was a young bride, and even in my thirties and forties, I never fully understood the importance of this kind of closeness between a man and a woman.

"One's body, one's soul, can be impoverished even while being well-fed, clothed, housed and physically adored! Without emotional intimacy, without the tenderness and touching, the talking – a woman dies a slow death. I believe that parts of her literally die off: cells, organs, and the natural rejuvenation of the life cycle! Or she internalizes her disappointment, and again, the void is like a deadly carrier of disease or a neurosis of some sort.

"Matt, what Stephen and I had was unique. We often spoke about it; about the seductive power of this phenomenon called 'spiritual affinity.' It was by far the most powerful emotion that I have ever known. There was a sensuality about it – a magnetic pull. We had an inordinate need to be with each other, a yearning to hear each other's voices – to share thoughts – that we simply could not suppress. I can still hear him say, 'I take great pleasure in just looking at you, Bess.' Or, 'How I love your face!'"

Matt sighed. "Ah, he is an astute man, all right, this Stephen Sohlberg! I want to meet him one day."

"Yes, you shall, my love," Bess promised. "Back then, Stephen and I would talk about the rarity of our relationship – how we could nourish each other, yet without carnal knowledge of one another. We hurt no one. Stephen underscored the need I had to exorcise myself from the stranglehold of sympathy for my husband without losing empathy. He empowered me to be in control of an otherwise intolerable situation. I, in turn, was his confidante – his 'consort,' he would laughingly say. He claimed that because of me, he had found greater meaning in his work.

"I took refuge in Stephen's office, which I later referred to as 'my hallowed sanctorium.' It was here that the 'calming of the waters' took place.

"Stephen once said that the love we had for each other was what all people crave in life. And that we had been blessed to find it without destroying any of our loved ones. I believe there lies the deepest desire – a compulsion, perhaps – to be understood by another human being. This force may even be more powerful than that of our sexual or hunger drives. Do you agree?"

"Yes, I've always thought that. But I just can't believe in all these years, you never made love," Matthew said incredulously.

"I suppose we did, Matt, but not in the usual sense. We made love by the way in which our eyes searched each other out, and once found, locked into one another. And there were the words – the spoken ones and those unspoken, as well. The extraordinary closeness and strength I drew from Stephen's presence was as if he were inside of me. We bared our souls, not our bodies. Together, Stephen and I, we slew the dragons of despair, even to the point of uncovering the demons within ourselves. Matt, it was Stephen who taught me that life has unending possibilities of renewal!

"Oh, Matthew, my darling man, I have been presented a second chance! Life *is* renewing itself for me. You and I have discovered one another before our time on this earth ceases to exist!"

MATTHEW SEEMED devoured by an uncontrollable desire to know every detail of Bess' so-called affair. He had become fixated. In his quest for Bess' absolute love and devotion, he delved further.

"What about his wife?" Matthew inquired.

"Sylvia, she has a disquieting presence – a kind of ruefulness," Bess volunteered. "You can see the tenseness in her posture. She's a thin-lipped woman – her mouth always seemingly pursed. Sylvia Sohlberg has an air of unapproachability about her – and a querulous nature. I had observed a coldness toward Stephen and their children which has caused Stephen much emptiness and pain.

"As we came to know one another, he expanded upon his marital disharmony, confirming my observations. But he was too honorable a man to leave her and their sons. Stephen was the backbone of that family! The children adored him – wouldn't have fared well without his daily presence!"

"Wasn't Stephen's sensitivity – or call it what you will – wasn't any of this evident when you met in college? Didn't you see it before you became engaged to David?" Matthew pondered out loud.

"Yes, I was attracted to Stephen before David came along. I gravitated to him, found his intellect impressive. We would often find ourselves in a corner at a party, talking politics or arguing various viewpoints and issues of the day. Both Stephen and I were from up North. We had a lot in common – our love of music and the arts.

"He had, or has, this exquisite sense of perception about what you're thinking or feeling or what you want to talk about. Many of my female friends at school loved to talk to him! He had such a depth of understanding, even then! But I wasn't physically attracted to him. I thought then, as young people do, that this chemistry thing was what really mattered. At age twenty, the hormones are kicking in. Remember? I wasn't thinking about what kind of man I would need some ten, twenty or thirty years hence.

"Stephen worked his way through school playing the piano. Although he was an excellent classical pianist, he performed jazz in local clubs, even driving his old jalopy to nearby towns on the weekends for a 'gig'. He was so good that the black clubs, which we referred to as 'joints' in those days, would invite him to 'jam' with them on many a weekend."

Matthew interrupted, "About David. Bess, I've wanted to ask you this for some time now. Didn't you notice anything unusual in his behavior during your courtship days? The manifestations of manic depression usually show up by then. There are telling signs – or indicators."

"Matt, remember how old I was when I met and fell in love with David? All of twenty! I saw a handsome man who loved me – who adored me. He came from a wonderful family and I was offered financial security for the first time in my life! I saw my parents struggle all of my youth; saw how worry over money eventually weakened their marriage. David was intelligent and had ambition. I didn't know then, in my youthful innocence, what mattered most.

"It wasn't until later in our marriage that I became aware of the torment which David suffered, both in mind and body. The serpent only reared its ugly head on occasion in those early years. I attributed the impatience, the irritability, the rancor, to sleep deprivation – endemic to physicians in David's specialty. A genetic abnormality or an aberration – the possibility of manic depression – never occurred to me, until I began checking into his mother's medical history."

"Was there passion between you and David – a bond other than with your children?" Matthew inquired.

"Oh yes, yes. We were very much in love for many years – throughout most of our marriage – until the last years when the drinking and despondency drew us apart. Our physical love – our sexual intimacy – had been a strong part of our marriage for a long time until even that came to an end," Bess responded quietly.

"You see, David eventually built a wall around himself that no amount of attentiveness or affection by me could penetrate. Physical love and sexual desire were then beyond him."

"Bess, do you still see Stephen – I mean, in therapy?"

"No, love, I haven't seen Stephen for almost a year now, not since you came into my life, my darling! But Stephen and I – we will remain friends. Can you handle that – now that you know about our 'spiritual' love affair?"

He thought for a long moment. "Yes, of course, I can handle it. In my mind, Stephen Sohlberg kept you going through great adversity. I owe him a debt of thanks!"

"Stephen and I talk on the phone occasionally and sometimes bump into each other at social occasions. Our families have been members of the same synagogue for years."

Bess then experienced a pinch of regret: "Oh, Matt, how I wish now that I hadn't told you all of this!"

"But Bess, I have to know about anyone who was or is close to you! So much of what you have told me – I mean, about Stephen and you, this 'spiritual affinity,' this emotional intimacy you shared – all of it just reinforces what I've known about you from the start – the depth of your soul – it's the extra dimension to you that I fell in love with!"

Still, Bess feared she had told him too much for one day. Better to have spaced it out – perhaps, over several days – even weeks or months. But she was not one to look back. It was done.

Matthew lifted Bess in his arms as she tightly held onto his shoulders, all the while kissing him over his face and into his neck as they made their way back to her bedroom.

They undressed each other slowly, admiringly. He told her that one day soon, when she felt ready to come to his home where he knew she would be less inhibited, he wanted to paint her. He loved the contours of her Rubenesque body. Today, he caressed every lovely curve. Then his tongue, his hands, his fingers made their way into each and every crevice.

Afterwards, she lay in Matthew's arms, bathed in the fluids of love and drenched with the sweat of their bodies. She asked him what satisfaction or enjoyment he derived from their lovemaking when he could not have an erection or ejaculation.

Matthew comforted Bess, explaining that when he brought her to fulfillment, when she cried out his name in love, he felt a completeness that he had rarely known in his lifetime.

They vowed this day never to leave each other – that somehow they would spend the rest of their lives together. Bess' mind raced ahead while Matthew explored aloud the plausibility of intertwining their lives. She knew the obstacles were formidable. There were reams of questions unanswered, like rough pills gathering in her throat. What would her children make of this unlikely union?

Her friends also – what would they think? Would

they regard Matthew Held simply as an amiable eccentric? But in the end, she knew it wouldn't really matter if they all disapproved. Someday, she would become Mrs. Matthew Held. They couldn't wait too long, though, as she realized in that moment. Her fifty-ninth year was soon approaching.

Only guard yourself and guard your soul carefully, lest you forget the things your eyes saw, and lest these things depart your heart all the days of your life. And you shall make them known to your children, and to your children's children.

Deuteronomy 4:9

CHAPTER FIVE

Sojourn

WE DIDN'T SHUT
off the ceiling fan, but instead let its oscillating movement blow gently over us. Lying next to each other, my
head nestled in the crook of Matthew's arm, we talked
endlessly.

What events had shaped who we were? Childhood
experiences are indelibly honed into our psyches. Could
we but mention them? Somehow understand their
impact upon our lives?

While I began to recount my trip to postwar
Europe as a young impressionable girl of thirteen,
Matthew sat up for a moment and lit a cigarette, then
tightened the covers around us, and propped himself up
on his elbow to look at me. I edged myself closer to
him and, knowing his ear for listening was intently in
place, I began my recollection of a time long ago when I
stepped beyond the innocence of childhood and walked
slowly, but surely, into the complexity of adulthood.

"IT WAS THE SUMMER of 1946. Under the
watchful eye of my grandfather, Asher Friedman, I was on

a European-bound ocean liner steaming toward the port of Bremerhaven, Germany.

"Aboard ship, but unbeknownst to Grandfather, I experienced the advent of menses. Fortunately our chambermaid Hilda, a brisk and efficient Dutchwoman, befriended me. Under her tutelage, I was shown how a woman copes with the necessary measures to keep herself clean and to camouflage the fact of her menstruation from others.

"I had my first crush on an 'older' man; one of the stewards. He was a blond, blue-eyed lad of seventeen. How I enjoyed, yet was confused by, the way in which he looked at me. His smile, that knowing stare, the rush of color to my cheeks – and Grandfather sensing the whole thing and having a talk with me about how I was forbidden to be alone with this 'older' man.

"Also during the voyage, I recall the horrifying sense that I was going to have only one developed breast. My right breast and nipple had swelled, yet nothing was occurring on the left side. The tenderness was like the dull pain of a toothache that I can summon up even now! I did not want to share this alarming discovery with Grandfather. Hilda knew enough to call in the ship's doctor who assured me I was developing in a normal, adolescent manner."

Reaching under the covers and placing his hands upon both my breasts, Matthew sighed, saying, "I believe the good doctor knew what he was talking about!" As I gently removed his hands, I spoke anew:

"Our trip had been planned for months. Grandfather convinced my parents, after much heated debate, that I would learn more during these off-school months in Europe, with him, than I would at an overnight summer camp.

"I was not made aware of the purpose of our journey until we had left the United States. We were to locate and bring home the lone Holocaust survivor of our family, one Harold Leichman, who had miraculously survived Bergen-Belsen and Auschwitz, two of the more notorious concentration camps.

"Grandfather had had only one communiqué from Harold during 1945 and the return address was Bergen-Belsen, Displaced Persons Camp, Block 8, Hamburg, Germany. But shortly before we left for Europe, through the efforts of our local Congressman, the International Red Cross and various refugee and relief agencies and the Hebrew Immigrant Aid Society (HIAS), word came to Grandfather that Harold was no longer at Bergen-Belsen. The authorities could not seem to find out which of the 30-odd displaced persons' camps Harold had gone to, or if he was in any of them at all.

"For all we knew, Harold could have gone home to Poland, or may have tried to reach Berlin where he had been a writer before the war. And too, Grandfather reasoned, perhaps Harold had become a Zionist, as had many refugees from the DP camps, and gone to Palestine which became the State of Israel in May of 1948: It was understandable that many of the refugees wanted to emigrate to Palestine, when the survivors heard of the unwelcoming conditions in their European community, the anti-Semitism that still flourished, the economy in ruin, their homes, businesses, temples and cities lying in rubble.

"Wherever we went, the authorities found Asher Friedman a force to be reckoned with. His resoluteness – his implacable will – gave me little doubt that if Harold Leichman were alive, Grandfather would find him.

"Even after V-E Day in Europe which celebrated

Victory in Europe, the Jewish displaced persons – DPs as they were referred to – could not indulge for very long in the euphoria of liberation, or of the vindication of good triumphing over evil. For in reality, the experiences of these Jews – these traumatized survivors – made it impossible for them to think and behave like other displaced persons. A vast gulf of agony and humiliation existed between them and the others. Eventually, Grandfather and I would see with our own eyes the prematurely aged and weak, and those suffering from extreme malnutrition.

"We had read in the reports that many thousands of Jews were at the very end of their strength by the time they were liberated, and died from the shock of liberation. Many died from the effects of eating food that their emaciated bodies were not able to metabolize. In fact, about forty percent of the Jewish DPs liberated in Germany perished within a few weeks *after* the arrival of the Allies.

"Though armed with this knowledge, we found ourselves unprepared for what we were to see. And this was in the summer of '46, a year after the war had ended and conditions in the DP camps had supposedly improved.

Bess continued, "But it would be much later in my life that I would fully comprehend the dimensions of horror created by Hitler's final solution and the suffering and hardship visited on my people. As a young thirteen-year-old, my perception then seemed more like a great adventure, even if somewhat frightening at times.

"The stench of dying – the combination of rubble mixed with the early summer warmth – all of this is embedded in my memory. Grandfather once wondered aloud: 'Were we 'chosen' for this – we, 'The Chosen People'?'

"At the Captain's table one evening aboard ship, other relatives of survivors questioned whether the Jewish people could ever hope to regain their spirituality – reclaim their heritage. They asked one another or thought out loud about Jewish culture and tradition. Could they be revived? How could Jewish identity in Eastern or Central Europe ever again hope to take root in the soil on which six million died?

"Others questioned whether synagogues and Hebrew Day Schools could rise again. Would the Jewish faith be stamped out forever, someone asked?

"I remember so well a lovely-looking older woman, who was going abroad to locate her sister who had stayed behind in Poland while she had left as a young girl to migrate to America. I have it marked; her words are in the diary that I kept of the trip. She spoke of the 'psychological misery and the ravaging of minds and bodies – of the human spirit.' She asked us, 'How can you revive something that is finished?'

"One gentleman answered her. 'If all the Jews leave, then Hitler will have achieved his desire to make that part of the world free of all Jews.' But yet another viewpoint was voiced. 'What will happen if the economy of Europe worsens? The Jews will be blamed once again. It could happen all over!'

"Toward the end of our journey, as we were soon to disembark, Grandfather spoke to all of us one evening, as the stony-faced stewards stood by, clanging the dishes, serving and removing the china, filling the water goblets over and over. 'The Jews of Persia survived the violent regime of King Ahasuerus. The Jews of Europe outlasted the Spanish Inquisition, and the Russian Empire could not wipe out the Jews with their pogroms. Hitler shall have lost as well. The Jewish people, above all else, are survivors!'

"As I retrace these events, I remember how proud I was of Grandfather. Although diminutive in size, he had a regal quality nonetheless – the straightness of his back – his measured words – his convictions shining brightly in those deeply-set grey eyes!

"Instead of the eighth-grade reading list I had been given in June of that summer and the corresponding books I brought aboard ship, I had sheafs of reports to read, supplied by my Grandfather. These had been given to him by HIAS, The International Red Cross and Jewish Refugee Organizations. Each day we would discuss the implications of these papers.

"There was one report I can still recount, which talked about the desperate conditions plaguing the war's survivors who lived among the more than thirty DP camps during July of 1945. On V-E Day, May 8, 1945, the DPs included two hundred thousand Jews – those who had somehow survived the forced-labor camps, concentration camps, extermination camps and the death marches.

"Even after two months of the war being over, the DPs were still wearing their old striped concentration camp uniforms because no other clothing had been issued them. The housing, medical and recreational facilities were inadequate and nothing was being done to improve their quality of life or to rehabilitate them. In 1945, no efforts were even being made to reunite families or to help survivors look for lost relatives.

"So, when word of these conditions leaked in the American press, President Truman sent Earl Harrison, former dean of the University of Pennsylvania Law School, on a fact-finding mission to the DP camps. The Harrison Commission found a lack of awareness of the traumatization suffered by the Jews. When he arrived, most were still living behind barbed wire in dozens of severely overcrowded former labor or concentration camps, together with non-Jewish DPs. They were guarded and were exposed to humiliating treatment and at times, to anti-semitic attacks. Nutrition, sanitary conditions and accommodations in the camps were poor, although they differed from one place to another."

Bess continued with her story: "I kept a summary of Harrison's findings folded within the pages of my diary. Here it is! Here is part of what he said in the report he sent to President Truman:

> *Three months after V-E Day, little has changed for the Jewish displaced persons. They remain in deplorable conditions, often crowded into the most notorious camps, without rehabilitation and with frequently mediocre care. As matters now stand, we appear to be treating the Jews as the Nazis treated them, except that we do not exterminate them. They are in concentration camps in large numbers under our military guard instead of SS troops. One is led to wonder whether the German people seeing this, are not supposing that we are following or at least condoning Nazi policy. The first and plainest need of these people is a recognition of their actual status, and by this I mean their status as Jews. To anyone who has visited the concentration camps and who has talked with the despairing survivors, it is nothing short of calamitous to contemplate that the gates of Palestine should be closed.*

Here Bess paused, and then slowly went on, "You see, Matthew, the struggle for a solution of the Jewish Displaced Persons' problem was part of the Zionist struggle for the immigration of the Jews to Palestine and for the establishment of a Jewish state there. Harrison was convinced that the only solution to the overall Jewish refugee problem was the emigration of the Jewish DPs to Palestine and so he recommended that the British be asked to issue, without delay, one hundred thousand entry permits or certificates, without waiting for the overall settlement of the Palestine question. The British declined the request.

"But the Harrison mission was a decisive turning point, both because of the effect it had on the living conditions of the DPs and because it resulted in President Truman's involvement in the struggle for the opening of the gates of Palestine.

"Apart from urging admission to Palestine for those Jews wanting to settle there, Harrison recommended that the United States and other countries should take some of the DPs as immigrants."

BESS WENT ON with her chilling story. "The DP chapter was slowly coming to an end at about the time Grandfather and I arrived in Europe. Eventually, with the establishment of the State of Israel in May of 1948, survivors living in the DP camps converged on Cyprus and Sicily to locate a seagoing convoy that would transport them to the Jewish state. Many of these vessels, after managing successfully to run the British Blockade, were later intercepted by British naval patrols. Once captured, the refugees were taken to Cyprus for internment.

"About two-thirds of the Jewish DPs made their way to Israel after a long and torturous struggle. The rest emigrated to the United States and other countries which at this time began to somewhat relax their immigration regulations.

"Banking on the considerable rise in sympathy for the Jewish DPs and refugees once the Harrison report had been made public, Truman instructed those in authority that America would admit displaced persons on a preferential basis. Between 1945 and 1946, about thirty thousand Jews had managed to enter the United States at a rate of about three thousand a month. Eventually, Harold Leichman would become one of these thirty thousand. But not before our long, exhausting, and often frustrating search had ended.

"Grandfather and I were met in Bremerhaven by a representative of HIAS who gave us an automobile, such as it was, and a driver, who spoke several languages. We were armed with a list of DP camps and their locations, and the possibilities of other locations where Harold may have been moved to.

"We were informed by HIAS that they had unearthed evidence that showed no one from Harold's family had survived the Holocaust. And all of Grandfather's relatives from Lodz, Poland, were gone as well! Asher Friedman accepted the news with an aura of resignation. He had never held out much hope, he later confided in me.

"We prayed that Harold's good sense would prevail and that he would not return to Lodz to seek out his family. Those who went back were confronted with catastrophic situations that they had not anticipated: Practically everyone they once knew had disappeared, and everything they once owned was destroyed or in other hands. Moreover, the stunned and bewildered Jews encountered massive hostility, particularly in Poland. Bitter quarrels ensued over apartments, or other property that had been plundered, stolen or confiscated. Pogroms anew took place across Poland, launched by right-wing extremists.

"After the worst genocidal attack in Jewish history, incredibly, a murderous anti-Semitism *still* continued, *even* after the war, *even* after the discovery of the horrific deeds committed by the Nazis.

"The most violent of these pogroms, as our driver informed us, occurred in the Polish town of Kielce, about two hundred kilometers south of Warsaw. This was not far from Lodz. Of the Jewish community of 250 persons in Kielce, a mob killed more than forty Jews and seriously injured many more, apparently with the help of local army units. We were later to learn that all told, 1,500 Polish Jews were murdered or died in pogroms between the end of World War II and 1946.

"The postmark on Harold's letter had said: Block 8, Bergen-Belsen Displaced Persons' Camp, Hamburg, Germany. On our way there, Grandfather showed me the letter he had received from Harold months after V-E Day. It was folded neatly but I could see by the creases that it had been read and reread many times. He kept it close, Grandfather did, in his breast pocket. Often I had seen him taking out the letter from the inside of his vest pocket. Placing his spectacles far down on his nose, as he always did when he read, he would study Harold's letter as if for the first time. Grandfather told me then of the convoluted journey across Europe and the United States that this misaddressed letter had taken. Grandfather asked me, but wasn't really expecting an answer (which was his pattern), what Harold must be thinking now since word of his whereabouts took so many months to find us in the United States. Did Grandfather's return letter to Harold take equally as long or did Harold ever receive it? Grandfather confided in me, 'I'm afraid Harold will think we do not wish to be bothered about getting him out of the camps or to settle him in the United States.'

"You see, from the day Grandfather received Harold's letter, it became his mission to get Harold into the United States. Although Grandfather wrote Harold that he would be coming to Europe and that he was obtaining the necessary affidavits, visas and so on, he never heard from Harold again. So we did not know if Harold knew we were coming, whether he knew and understood of Grandfather's commitment.

"Bergen-Belsen, now a displaced persons' camp, once a former concentration camp, was located in lower Saxony, in northern Germany, near the city of Celle. It was not far from Hamburg, where we stopped for directions. Here we found surviving Jews from different countries with diverse cultural and social traditions who were building themselves a temporary home in which, we were told, within a few short months after V-E Day, began to develop into an organized Jewish community. As we went through the 'blocks' at Bergen-Belsen, we heard dance rhythms of the horah, people singing Yiddish and Hebrew songs, and others peering into an ancient Jewish text that had just come into the camp. We were told by one of the British liberators, who was taking us through the camp, that although weak from malnutrition and broken in body and spirit when the British first liberated Bergen-Belsen, most of the surviving Jews derived strength in their priority of feeding, caring for, and educating the children. The healing of the sick, the clothing of the naked, became urgent and constructive tasks for the survivors. The British commander told us how the Jews organized themselves into committees soon after the liberation to see that a more equitable distribution of food took place. Others opened schools or organized and printed newspapers and established religious activities. 'These were priorities for the survivors and gave them a reason to live,' I recall our British guide saying. Unfortunately, not all of the survivors lived to enjoy their freedom. Many had died from epidemic sicknesses during the very days that the news broke through that 'the sun was still shining.' Many, with damaged minds and bodies, overcome by months and years of malnutrition, could not muster the strength to go on, even though now freed.

Bess' eyes filled again with tears. "As a young girl, I found it difficult to look at the survivors, at least in the beginning. Their eyes were downcast or focused somewhere beyond. Some smiled toothless half-smiles: the Germans had pulled out teeth that contained gold fillings. Others had lost their teeth or dentures because of the decay within their bodies. There was a nervous pulsing around the mouth. Some of the women smiled demurely, while others – self-conscious of their worn and tattered clothing and skeletal bodies – barely reacted to our presence. Several, I remember, made nervous gestures with their hands.

"Some had eyes like pieces of coal while others had a hollowed-out or haunted look. I felt as if I could see through their eyes as if they were clear marbles. And their voices! How can I explain after all these years, the almost-inaudible, strange sounds emanating from their wretched bodies – their agonizing memories?

"While meeting with leaders of the various Jewish committees and the head of the British Liberation Team to discuss with them the possible whereabouts of one Harold Leichman, we could not help but notice emissaries from the Palestine Brigade. Particularly impressive to Grandfather and me were the automobiles of the Brigade, decorated with blue and white Stars of David and fluttering with the blue and white flags of the soon-to-be State of Israel. We could see with our own eyes how the Brigade exalted the spirit of the Jewish survivors. The Star of David symbol, which the Nazis had degraded by turning it into a yellow patch, served now to strengthen the national consciousness of the survivors. It was the Zionist Brigade from Palestine that came early on to inspect the conditions in the DP camps and to make recommendations to the various refugee organizations and Allied liberators.

"Where possible, the Brigade set up schools to teach adults and children about Palestine, with special focus on the agricultural needs of the Promised Land. For this new country, from the moment of its birth, would need many hands to toil the hardened desert earth – to help it become a land of plenty. One could see then how the idea of starting a new life in another land was the healing grace for many survivors. It was the survivors' spirit of renewal that so impressed Grandfather and me.

"Under military orders of General Eisenhower, U.S. aircraft transported teachers, instructors and books from Palestine to the DP camps. Regular postal and other forms of communication between survivors and families anywhere in the world was established by military order. Eisenhower also authorized the appropriate authorities to provide the Jews with a certain number of agricultural facilities for use as training schools for young people. This was begun in October of 1945.

"Finally, we received news of Harold! We learned that while languishing in the DP camp in Bergen-Belsen, he had become quite ill. He could not seem to digest food after having been near starvation for so many months. And he had been kicked so often and hard in the groin area that he had developed urological problems. We found his name on a waiting list to be admitted to the medical DP camp at St. Ottilien, near Munich.

"The St. Ottilien convent had been taken over by the DPs themselves and had become a hospital for the more severely-ill displaced persons from other DP camps. And yes, we discovered that Harold had indeed been at St. Ottilien. They had done all they could for him. The

DP committee at St. Ottilien felt strongly that he had become a Zionist and was making his way to either Italy or Cyprus to find space on a boat bound for Palestine. Grandfather sent a wire to HIAS in Palestine but there was no record of a Harold Leichman, emigré.

"We had also been told by our British guides that many of the more displaced persons who were severely ill, both physically or psychologically, had been transported from Bergen-Belsen to Sweden. Sweden had offered to take in several thousand Jewish survivors. Grandfather contacted the Swedish consul, through HIAS, but there was no word of a Harold Leichman in Sweden, either.

"We were informed that Harold had helped hundreds of DPs, both at Bergen-Belsen and at St. Ottilien, to compose letters to family members in the United States and other countries, and he had begun the newspaper at Bergen-Belsen, which soon became the model for all other DP camps. Because Harold spoke five languages, his skills as an interpreter had made him useful to the Nazis both at Auschwitz and Bergen-Belsen, and probably accounted for his still being alive after the war.

"We met survivors at Bergen-Belsen who told us of Harold's burgeoning interest in Zionism, but we still wanted to cover all possibilities. So we visited as many DP camps as possible. In Germany, we went to camps in Landsberg, Feldefing, Zeilsheim, Fernwald, Munich, Hannover, Stuttgart, Bremen, Kassel, Braunsweig, Bamberg and Regensburg. I hated the sound of the camp names. The evil ring each one held for me still evokes a shuddering of fear.

"A building in Heilbroon, Germany had been hit by an aerial bomb just weeks before becoming a displaced persons camp, yet was deemed sufficient housing for the refugees. Another camp at Lingen, Germany was an indescribably filthy structure where there was inadequate food, personnel and medical supplies. We were told by many DPs that living conditions in the majority of the DP camps were primitive and that they initially existed solely on rations of bread and coffee.

"In 1945, the DP camps were often transitory. The DPs themselves moved frequently, searching for family members, despite official warnings and military guards. They followed the Nazi-installed lamp posts, telephone wires and telephone poles. Sometimes the DPs moved on orders from the authorities because of overcrowding or epidemics of typhus.

"We saw taped-up photos of missing family members, and messages scrawled upon the walls of reception centers. The DPs and even those in authority referred to the writing on the walls as 'wailing walls' or 'agony columns.'

"When Grandfather and I heard that HIAS had just opened a branch office in Lodz, we proceeded there on the chance that Harold had gone home where his family had been highly regarded by both the Jewish and Gentile communities before the war.

"In an entry of my diary, I have recorded Grandfather's words as we stepped off the train and made our way to the main square in Lodz. 'This looks like the end of the world, not just the end of the war,' Grandfather remarked, his voice breaking off now and then, but keeping his emotions in check. He talked as if no one was with him. He could scarcely bring himself to look at me. 'The bright skies of my childhood days – the sweet smell of the flowers – the cleanliness of the people – the streets – the humming sounds of the businesses – the pleasant nod of the proprietors – it is all gone – they are no more. The people – those who remain – they are grey, like the few buildings that still stand.'

"As we looked around we saw the faces of those who were left. They were the elderly, the weak and those too poor to emigrate. Grandfather's childhood home had been obliterated by the Nazis and it, along with hundreds of others, lay in a heap of rubble.

"Grandfather walked on as if in a daze. That day is sharply etched in my memory. The village lay quiet in an early evening rain. Through the mist, we saw, outlined against the sky, what remained of Grandfather's sisters' home. All that stood were the wrought iron gates. And yet, a few flowers protruded from the high weeds. He placed one in his lapel and the others he entwined in my hair, twisting the stems into each of my braids. He put his arms around me and held me close. I still recall how the rough tweed of his jacket felt against my cheeks and how they absorbed my tears.

"I slid my arm through his, sensing there were no right words that I could comfort him with. Not now, not yet. But I knew then why I had come this far; why he had selected me of all the family to come with him. He knew I would carry on the family tradition – that I would never, not ever – after seeing all I had seen and knowing all I had come to know – ever stop being a Jewess. But I knew that even this wasn't enough. I would go home with a greater sense of purpose as a Jew – and all these millions of Jews deprived of their right to be a Jew – being tortured or killed simply because they were born a Jew – would forever become a bond with me – they did not die in vain. I would somehow carry *their* Jewishness in my soul and keep it alive.

"We were traveling by train now on our way back to Germany from Poland when Grandfather looked up at me over dinner and said he wanted to go back to Bergen-Belsen to talk to some of Harold's friends to perhaps gain a better understanding of what Harold may have been thinking and talking about or planning. And so we retraced our steps and journeyed toward Hamburg.

"When we arrived at Bergen-Belsen, several of the survivors came running toward us, shaking our hands, speaking excitedly, acting quite emotional. At first we thought they were simply happy to see us. On our first visit, Grandfather had brought all kinds of care packages from the States, such as hosiery, candy, socks, shaving supplies, perfume, books, and the like. So we thought they were just pleased to see their newest benefactor. But one of the men, who spoke a broken English, said that Harold had returned to Bergen-Belsen. We couldn't believe our ears. We wept with joy! They wept along with us!

"When we were brought to Block Eight, a place Harold called 'home,' we were stunned. Of course I had known Harold would be very thin and gaunt. But he seemed aged for a man of twenty-eight. His hair was very grey and he was bearded. I thought to myself how he resembled one of the biblical prophets. Sitting beside him on his cot was a beautiful woman, fair-haired and blue-eyed. Her hand rested upon his. They rose to greet us, extending their arms, tears glistening on their faces. "Uncle, this is my wife, Hannah Goldfarb Leichman." We all embraced. A chair appeared from nowhere for Grandfather.

"We listened intently as Harold talked in his halting English, 'I was at Auschwitz where, because I knew several languages, I was deemed valuable to the Nazis as an interpreter at the camp's textile factory. When the Germans heard rumors that the Russians were advancing, they announced we were leaving the camp on a long march. With only blankets and rags to cover our bodies, and the combination of cold, snow, hunger and disease, it was a death march for all but sixty of 500 people. Most of us got typhus. Others had the dysentery. The farmers in the countryside felt sorry for us and, despite warnings not to help us, tried to get food to us. Parts of my body were frostbitten, and most of my body was swollen and purple. Eventually we were loaded onto trucks for we could no longer walk. Then we were put on freight trains bound for Bergen-Belsen.

"'One morning while here at Bergen-Belsen, when the Gestapo usually came to count the prisoners to see who was still alive, no one came. We heard voices that the Nazis had left the camp. My brethren were screaming with both agony and joy, running to the kitchens to find food. But I was totally helpless, lying in the damp grass with a high fever, unable to go to the kitchen with some of the others. Two of my friends brought back food to me, but I was too weak to eat, so they finished it all. Within one hour, they, and all those who had eaten from the kitchen, were dead. The Gestapo had poisoned the food before running away.

"'Soon the Red Cross jeeps arrived with British officers to distribute food and water, yelling 'We bring you freedom!' But there was only hysteria, everyone screaming. We had lost our families. The British were not prepared for the hopeless physical condition of the survivors they found. They thought, at first, that we were merely lying down, resting. More people died because they couldn't handle the food. Hospital wards were quickly set up in the Nazi quarters. We were cleaned, deloused and given lengthy rehabilitation. Much of the medicine, food and clothing came from your country, dear Uncle.

"'Many of the more able-bodied male Jewish youngsters went to hunt SS men in the bars during the early days of the liberation. We tried to talk them out of it, but they pushed us aside. The SS had tattoos under their armpits as identification and were easily identifiable, even though many tried to hide by wearing prisoner uniforms. When the boys found them, they turned them over to the Americans or the British, but not until after they had beaten them up.

"'After leaving here, I made my way to the convent at St. Ottilien. The authorities here at Bergen-Belsen had placed me at the bottom of the sick list. I couldn't wait. I knew I would die if I didn't receive more specialized treatment right away. It was a prophetic decision on my part, for it was at St. Ottilien that I became whole again physically and it was there that I met Hannah.' He reached out and placed his arm around her. 'We tried to get to Palestine after the recuperation. We made it to Sicily to wait for a boat, but no boats came, so we hitchhiked back to Germany – back here to Bergen-Belsen. For it was from here that I had written you, Uncle, in the earliest days of the Liberation, and we hoped that eventually you would find us, here.'"

BESS' STORY TO MATTHEW continued, as her voice had taken on a calmness: "It was then that Grandfather introduced me to Hannah and Harold. Harold rose and kissed me on both cheeks and smiled beneficently. Hannah took me by the hand and guided me to her cot. 'Shane, a shana' she said over and over, while stroking my braids, informing me that she, too, had worn her hair like mine when she was thirteen. (*Shane* means beautiful in Hebrew.) Then Grandfather asked Hannah to tell her story, and she spoke in surprisingly good English.

"She told us that she, Hannah Goldfarb, had been born and raised in Radom, Poland. She and her sister were separated from their family when their village found out that the Nazis were coming to take them to the camps. Many of Radom's Jews, ten thousand in all, were systematically shot at point-blank range in Radom's town square. Hannah and her younger sister were hidden in a convent and, because of their blue eyes and blonde hair, no German suspected that they were Jewish.

"They lived there 'til the end of the war. Her parents were gassed at Auschwitz, she later was to learn. She and her sister wore the habit of the Sisters and therefore did not arouse suspicion from various Nazi regiments and SS troops who periodically made their rounds of inspection looking for Jews hiding in rafters, the basement or eaves of the convent. They turned the convent upside down and the Reverend Mother, said Hannah, dreaded their visits. But Reverend Mother, Hannah recounted, maintained her demeanor at all times as well as the other nuns. When the war was over, Hannah, who had been trained as a nurse, asked the Allied authorities to let her work in the DP camps that were specializing in medical treatment for the more seriously ill. She was soon transferred to the convent at St. Ottilien which comprised some of the best medical treatment for DPs throughout Europe.

"As Hannah spoke, I looked at Harold and saw the pride in his face. They had been married at Bergen-Belsen and showed us the handmade marriage symbols that some of the survivors had made for their wedding. Hannah brought out her wedding dress, constructed from her white nurse's uniform sewn together with the habit she had saved from her convent days.

"Their love and subsequent marriage took on a special meaning in a place like Bergen-Belsen that had known only misery and death. Rebirth and renewal –

these two words I recall Harold using frequently in his talks with Grandfather and me.

"He never told us very much of his suffering in the concentration camps, nor did he speak of the great tragedy befallen his family and the Jewish people. Although he was at times lethargic and emaciated in appearance, I do not remember either he or Hannah ever speaking with bitterness. Then, as now, I see their focus on the goodness and courage of man, and eternal hope. But as I retrace their story I do recall Harold speaking of the awareness of the homelessness which he and Hannah felt profoundly, and their sense of dislocation.

"Harold found incomprehensible the shocking apathy of the international community for the plight of the Jewish people. Harold told Grandfather that later in the war, the Allies knew full well of the killing and torturing in the camps and could have at least bombed the railroad tracks leading to and from the camps.

"Even years later, when Harold had become well-versed in the historical background of that time and place, he could never quite accept the rationale that the Allies' refusal to carry out such a bombing was due to the military and diplomatic implications of the impending European invasion."

The stranger that sojourneth with you shall be unto you as the home-born among you, and thou shalt love him as thyself.

Leviticus XIX – 34

CHAPTER SIX

Sojourn's End

BEFORE WE COULD
leave Europe for the United States, Grandfather had to
perform a few other miracles – like secure a visa and
other affidavits for Hannah. We had only booked passage
on the return trip for Grandfather, myself and Harold.
We had not known about Harold having a wife. We had
to extend our trip and rebook passage on another ocean
liner, now that we needed four tickets. But within two
weeks, Grandfather had managed to secure the necessary
documents for Hannah to accompany us to the States.

"Grandfather also wired my parents to ask them
permission to allow Hannah and Harold to stay at our
home for a few months until he, Grandfather, could find
them an apartment and jobs in New York City. They
wanted to live in a big city where many of their survivor
friends had congregated, and Harold, as a writer, needed
to find work on a metropolitan newspaper.

"When we finally arrived home, my parents couldn't
believe how much I had matured. Embracing them warmly,
I had this sudden realization of having gone a step beyond
'their little girl.' I felt older, wiser. Soon the discovery of

being somewhat apart from my peers would descend upon me as well.

"Hannah and Harold were shy and quiet. At times this made my parents feel uneasy. They thought they should be doing more for their beloved guests. Somehow, even as a young girl, I knew that Hannah and Harold simply could not bring themselves to speak of the unspeakable.

"I remember explaining to my parents that it was only natural that Harold was always looking over his shoulder. It would be a while until Harold's suspicion and fear of others would subside. He had to learn to trust again, and eventually he did. This was all part of the conditioning from living in such a place as a concentration camp, where one's inability to comprehend or differentiate who would turn on you for an extra slice of bread (usually for a loved one) or a respite from hard labor (also to save a loved one) could mean your life.

"When Harold and Hannah tried to eat a normal amount of food, at least in the beginning weeks, their stomachs would balloon or enlarge. Sometimes they were actually sickened by the vision of so much abundance. They would politely excuse themselves from the table and go to their room. I don't think my parents ever completely understood what they were feeling. The cousins were reticent to talk about what they had either witnessed or experienced themselves. They broke into tears easily, fell apart when there was a knock at the door, froze when a large black car would appear. The recollection of a black car, coming in the middle of the night to take away a friend or a family member to the camps, was still a vivid memory.

"Grandfather secured a position for Harold in New York City on a Jewish newspaper that was printed in German, Polish and Yiddish. The only job he could find for Hannah was as a Hebrew teacher, but she was grateful for the opportunity, as they both were. Years later, after their children were in school, Hannah acquired a nurse's license from the state of New York, and worked for many years at Mt. Sinai Hospital."

"Are they alive?" Matthew asked, breaking his silence for the first time.

"Yes, Matt. They're in their eighties and although suffering from various ailments, are fairly self sufficient. We have always maintained a close relationship. Over time David and I would visit with them in their home, and they, here."

Bess was finally back in the here-and-now, and she turned her attention to Matthew. "Oh, my love, did I put you to sleep with my long dissertation?"

"No," Matthew said, "I closed my eyes several times, to try and picture you there, alongside your Grandfather. I have been trying to visualize Hannah and Harold and...."

"I was forever changed by this experience – you know this, darling, don't you?"

"Yes, Bess. I know. And my not being Jewish – is this another obstacle that will stand in our way?"

"No, Matt, I won't let it!"

"Do you want me to convert? I will, you know, if that's what you want."

"Just like that? When you know so little of our religious traditions, our culture, and...?"

"If my being Jewish is important to you Bess, I will be Jewish!"

"Someday, maybe, Matthew, but not now – no – not yet. Over time, you will witness for yourself the strength and beauty of my Judaism, and then, and only then, if you study, and you still decide you want this for yourself. All right?"

"Yes, if that's the way you wish it."

"Yes, Matt, that's the way I wish it. And the subject of your possible conversion is closed for now. Agreed?"

"Yes."

Matthew reflected out loud, "You know, when I lived in Brooklyn, in an old brownstone walk-up on Flatbush Avenue, down the street there was a combination candy store and ice cream parlor run by the Ackermans. Once, when I was helping Mr. Ackerman pick up a heavy delivery order, his sleeve that was rolled up, pushed up farther back, and I saw the numbered tattoo on his forearm. Mr. Ackerman stopped what he was doing to pull his sleeve down. I saw the embarrassment – the way he looked me in the eye. I felt for him."

"Yes," Bess spoke reflectively, "the eight violet colored digits inside the forearm crying aloud the Reich's inhumanity and its obsession with recordkeeping."

"What about your childhood, Bess? Were you raised in a Jewish home?"

"My parents were indifferent in the attention they paid to the Jewish rituals. And I, before my European odyssey, was somewhat irreverent in my own attitude and behavior toward my Judaism. My parents were not observant Jews, though they attended synagogue services on the High Holy Days. But that was about it. We even hung stockings at the fireplace at Christmas while still celebrating Chanukah! But when I returned from Europe, my attitude had changed. I insisted that we observe the Sabbath with candle lighting, blessings over the bread and the wine. And I went to our Temple to pray on Saturday mornings or Friday evenings several times a month. Sometimes my parents would come along with me. Other times, they just dropped me off, until I could drive myself. Later on, I found a few people my own age that felt the importance of being grounded in one's faith. And for many years, I had the pleasure of accompanying Grandfather to synagogue.

"And when I married David, who was somewhat detached from his Jewishness, and moved to this small southern community where being Jewish was even more difficult, I found ways to keep my faith for myself and our children. But it was never easy. By then, though, it had become second nature to me. My faith is like my right arm. I would find life far more agonizing without it or the beliefs I hold dear. And through the torment of David's illness and his death, my religion was my ally – a trusted friend. It has carried me through some dark times, Matt!"

"And Stephen being Jewish, I mean, the both of you share this sense of heritage – this oneness," Matthew remarked, staring out the window.

"I can't deny that, Matt. Yes, I'm sure the fact that we are both Jewish – and share a common bond – and Stephen so well-versed in the undergirding of Judaism, added to our closeness. We spent hours discussing and working through Jewish attitudes toward illness and death. Yes, there is no doubt that this had a profound bearing on our relationship.

"But enough about me, my religion, Stephen, Europe! Let's talk about us... Hold me, Matthew, and promise to never let me go – never let me out of your life, my darling man!"

He held her close to him. They didn't make love that day, but held tightly to one another, talking for hours – speaking only briefly of their desire to spend the rest of their lives together. Soon they found themselves outside, out in the garden, side-by-side, on bended knee.

CHAPTER SEVEN

Alex

I AM THE OLDEST
grandchild and only grandson of Bess Cantin, two facts of
which I have been mindful from my earliest memories.

At a moment's notice, I can conjure up Nana's
determined expression as she threads a live worm onto
the end of my fish hook. She carries along her writing
materials, folding chair, and shoulder-strapped thermos. I
bring up the rear with not one, but two fishing poles that
are housed at Carlisle Way. I bring two rods because I'm
still prone to jamming reels.

We sit on the edge of the pier for hours. There isn't
much talking. I'm a dedicated fisherman right from the
beginning, and I know Nana relishes the quiet.

Now and then, out of the corner of my eye, I sense
she is looking at me with that proud expression of hers,
which I knew was reserved solely for me, and on occasion,
my sister, Amy!

If I catch anything at all – a croaker if I'm lucky,
sometimes a crab by mistake – Nana shares in my
excitement, helping me deposit the creature in an old
coffee can (with ice packs) that she keeps 'specially for

these fishing "expeditions."

When the tide was low or "they weren't swimming" as Nana would say, I'd take a special pole with a fine gauge net at its end and "capture" minnows or mussels, which I was gently prodded to return to their rightful home when it was time to leave.

Evenings at Carlisle Way, we'd play Monopoly or gin rummy, usually my choice! Nana was, and is, a fine gin rummy player by any standard, and the skills of this game, if cogently applied, she often says, parallel life. Her line goes something like: "Gin Rummy *is* life, for the hand you're dealt is rife with possibilities."

When I was seven, it was Nana who taught me to ride a bicycle without training wheels at a nearby park, where all five-foot-two inches of her would push me with all her might while I pedaled furiously to stay straight on the large, grassy portion of the field. "Alex," she'd shout enthusiastically after me, "keep going – that's it – you've got it! Keep pedaling! You have wings, Alex! Fly!"

It was in Nana's four-legged old bathtub at Carlisle Way where I first learned to swim. I was three, maybe four, when she showed me how to face float, or in her day as she termed it, a "dead-man's" float. After I mastered this step, she began taking me to the club pool where at its shallow end, Bess Cantin, unconcerned about how others might view her, began dog-paddling and blowing bubbles with me until I caught on.

I think determination is Nana's middle name. If she thought Amy or I needed to learn something, she would teach it to us, or find someone who could.

How to explain this earnest woman with her unspoken moral strength, inner calm and laser-like directness? She is remarkably candid. Some members of our family think her too forthright – emboldened. But you always know where you stand with Nana.

Although her attributes are many, Nana is not without foible or flaw. To some she may appear strident when her zealousness over a cause or a person takes hold. Bess Cantin cannot abide gossip, idleness or small talk. Her patience wears thin when confronted with complainers, malingerers or parasites. And she has an aversion to long-winded telephone calls!

She has a way of judging people or things both rationally and emotionally – almost simultaneously. As children, Amy and I felt impelled to tell her of our disappointments or problems. She sagaciously replied with some kind of empathetic remark. But because Nana looked life straight in the eye, soberly embracing its ambiguities and dilemmas, she resisted placating us with undue concern, sentimentality or emotional stroking.

Gently but firmly, Nana expressed how we must not let querulous people or unpleasant events define us. We had to rise above minutiae or the ineffectiveness or weaknesses of others. Nana often took our thoughts and turned them inside out. If we tried to blame our failures on others, she was quick to remind us that in life, all you have is what you make of the talents God gives you, pointing out various world leaders or exemplary citizens who rose above humble beginnings, physical handicaps, neglectful or absent parents, to go on to achieve greatness or who contributed to bettering the human condition.

Over the protestations of my mother and several family members, Matthew Held became Nana's lover and eventually, her husband. Nana and Matthew married when Nana was nearly sixty years old.

Their love affair and marriage caused a considerable stir in the circles of our family and friends. It was more class snobbery, at least in my mind, than anything else.

But what the human soul yearns for, a degree of stubborn willfulness can accomplish. As the story of their relationship unfolded, it was obvious – to anyone who could search out the truth, – that their lives were now fused. Never before had Nana been so tranquil. There was a decade of living separating them, religious differences, class distinctions, monetary imbalances – but their love for each other was ennobling; inspirational.

As a young boy, I was searching for a hero. My grandfather, David Cantin, whom I had loved and admired, died when I was twelve. My own father was in D.C., or overseas a good deal of the time.

Vividly etched in my memory upon first viewing Matthew Held was his grin and easy manner. He never seemed to be in a hurry, yet he was constantly in motion; painting, fixing, planting, and the like. I used to wonder how he could be so happy driving an old beat-up car, wearing clothes that looked like hand-me-downs, and never going to the best concert, play or sporting event, nor eating at the best restaurants.

I would intentionally bring up these disparities in conversation, perhaps lauding them as children are prone to do, but more, I think, to test his mettle or the sincerity of his beliefs. I soon realized he didn't give a hoot if he saw the latest flick or dined on venison! He bore none of the affectations one associates with success or the strivings of those trying to reach there.

As time wore on, Nana showed me some of Matt's art work and told me of his background. I soon became aware of the unique qualities of this multi-faceted male being. More importantly, I began to see Matthew Held through the eyes of my grandmother. This early spring squall, the winding old roads that I deliberately take on my drive home to Carlisle Way, do not divert my thoughts of Bess and Matthew.

Their love is unlike any other I have so far observed. Each has reached down into themselves, searched, and without surrendering their own uniqueness, become whole. Each has become something unto himself. Each possesses something uniquely his own, yet their desire for each other, once realized, seems to have fulfilled them completely. External happenings do not matter. As Nana's favorite poet, Rainer Marie Rilke said, "A warm, tender, touching concern evolved, making them more in their union than they would have become if they had each chosen to live alone."

My attention veers inexorably back to the dilemma Nana faced when she revealed the love she shared with Matthew. How well I remember her talk with me about how Matthew was the embodiment of all that is good and loving in man! She sat with my mother and me and told us how she drew strength from Matthew. She told us that Matthew was a man of rare intelligence who valued *being* as much as *doing,* and knew life was equal parts joyful and absurd. That he possessed the secret to the serenity of the simple life. That he, like her, found something divine in wind, sky and water. And that neither of them were patient with small talk or stupidity and had endless compassion for clarity.

I often, as now, retrace the genesis of my own philosophy of love which more than likely evolved from many talks with Nana and my own observations of this unusual couple. This is what I recall so well about Nana's words to me about herself and Matthew:

"Alex, Matthew and I – we love who we are; what we do. And ours is a most uncommon love – we speak with one voice. As Socrates wrote in *The Phaedrus*, 'may the outward and inward man be at one.' Matthew's inner harmony, my darling Alex, his grace, has overshadowed whatever differences there were."

DR. DAVID CANTIN was a respected cardiologist and surgeon – saver of lives and my mentor while my own father was absent a good part of my childhood. Although my grandfather kept long hours, whether it was attending to his patients, working out at the gym or manipulating his funds through a high-wire act of financial juggling at Merrill-Lynch, somehow he found a few hours each week to spend with me, one-on-one. He taught me how to read and follow the stock market index. In fact, on each birthday, from the day of my birth, David Cantin purchased stocks in my name which he managed to parlay into enough money to pay most of my medical school expenses.

He was a well-respected, larger-than-life kind of man; broad-shouldered, with a large receding forehead, steely blue eyes that could dress you down or lift you up at whim, and the robust look of an outdoorsman (from his many hours on the links!). He did not countenance the fluctuating moods or mores of the times. He was truly a traditional man and, although non-indulgent with Amy and me (and Nana), and undemonstrative in his affections with us all, we knew he kept us close to his heart.

I did not know until long after his death, when Nana felt I was mature enough to hear the truth, that Dr. David Cantin was a manic-depressive, an alcoholic the last twenty years of his life and a suicide. The medical community, grandfather and grandmother's closest friends and our extended family, all were unaware of his suicide – so well-kept was Nana's secret and "cover-up."

"Your grandfather was a good man, Alex, and I would not have his reputation sullied," Nana had explained.

In my youth, I was often witness to grandfather's dark and brooding moods; his highs and lows. I knew he suffered from insomnia and that he downed too many pre-dinner high-balls. Soon after his body had absorbed the alcohol, within thirty minutes or so, his mood would change into either one of despair or despondency. Although I never saw David Cantin become violent, there was a rawness to his verbal bite – an edginess in his tone – a kind of bridling, especially when he drank.

Once I recall asking Nana if Grandpa David was angry with me. I still remember her answer. "He loves you very much, Alex. He loves us all. Your grandfather just works too hard!" I never bought it all, but I knew the subject was closed and that Bess Cantin was dealing with it as best she could.

IT IS SPRING BREAK and I have chosen to spend it at Carlisle Way, visiting with Nana and Matthew. Some of the guys are taking their R&R down in Lauderdale or San Juan. Jan has gone home to visit with her folks and to plan our wedding. We will be married in the fall. Nana and Matt have offered to host both the ceremony and reception at Carlisle Way. We have accepted gladly.

My parents divorced during my pre-med days. Dad spends more and more time in Europe, now that he has an assistant secretarial position with State. Mom works in DC as a legislative liaison for our local Congressman. And Amy is in DC also, studying for her masters in International Diplomacy at GW.

Bess and Matthew have been husband and wife for almost sixteen years now, with Nana saying she is seventy-six years young and Matthew admitting, rather reluctantly, to being sixty-four or "thereabouts."

Mother says Nana is not feeling up to par and that

she seems to have less energy and takes to her bed quite often, which is not like her at all. But I tried to reassure Mother, reminding her of Nana's age. Yet, I worry, too. For in my last telephone conversation with Matthew, his voice seemed a bit strained as he tried to reassure me of Nana's good health.

It is dusk now. I've exited off the main road, slowly winding my way around the secondary roads that will eventually bring me to Carlisle Way. The green nubs of spring are everywhere.

With the arrival of Matthew Held to Carlisle Way, small miracles happened. Between his knowledge of grafting and cuttings – the seeding of bulbs and corm, he brought to Carlisle Way the sweet scent of life which he gently extracts and lifts from the earth.

Carlisle Way looked somewhat different to me as I approached its circular driveway, taking note of Matthew's well-manicured lawn and shrubbery. Ivy had traversed the cream-colored façade in a spidery, haphazard manner, lending an aura of an old English vine-covered cottage.

"She's becoming quaint, like me!" Nana called out as she walked with a certain hesitancy toward my car. The exuberance I had fondly remembered about her was replaced by a slower, more cautious gait which unsettled me. She had quipped, "Carlisle Way and Bess Cantin have some barnacles in common these days, Alex, love!"

We embraced heartily as always. As I held her a moment longer than I thought she wished, I could feel that her body lacked the muscle-bound frame as before. Suddenly there was this fragility about her.

"Is Matt around, Nana?" I asked as I let her go, smiling through my concern, but not fooling her for an instant.

"He's in the study with Stephen Sohlberg. You

remember Stephen?"

"Yes, of course. Dr. Sohlberg. You two are old friends."

"Well, now he's become Matthew's friend as well! Or should I say, they are fast becoming friends. And he's tutoring Matthew in Judaism for conversion!"

I had known of Matt's interest in Judaism. He had often remarked that one day, when time permitted, he would like to study the precepts of Nana's faith. Matthew had witnessed firsthand the strength Nana derived from her Jewishness.

"Why not the Rabbi, Nana – why Stephen?"

"Well, the Rabbi only comes to town now for Sabbath services about twice a month, splitting his time with another synagogue in Waverly. It's a shame, Alex, but our Jewish community is dwindling. Well, anyway, Stephen is considered the most knowledgeable lay leader in our community. Besides which, his closeness to your grandfather and to me makes this an especially unique experience, don't you agree?"

"I see, sure, it makes sense," I nodded in agreement.

As we talked some more about the course of study planned for Matthew both by the Rabbi and Stephen, I saw that Nana did not wish to allow too much excitement in her voice about Matt's impending conversion, or the fact that Stephen and Matthew were getting to know one another, which she desperately desired.

"I'll go and check on dinner, Alex." She hugged me again, "just for good measure" she said, as always, on that second hug. And as in my teen years or for that matter, in these latter years, I pulled on her apron string and "in-her-face," retorted, "Don't press your luck, lady!" Then we broke up in laughter. Our affectionate jostling was a natural part of our relationship; had been so since I was a young child.

Off she went, and as Matt approached the car, an air of apprehension hung about him as if in anticipation of questions I would surely pose concerning Nana's health. The thinning grey hair had receded somewhat and served to accentuate his furrowed brow. But it is the eyes that mirror the heart. And as I eyeballed Matthew Held, I became acutely aware of the precariousness of Bess Cantin's hold on life.

As Matt puffed on a stogie (his concession to Bess' aversion to cigarettes), I could detect from the non-verbal cues he was giving off his distaste at being a harbinger of doom.

"HOW'S IT GOING, Alex?" Matthew inquired, while embracing Alex with a bear-hug.

"Life's treating me well, Matt. Med school's going great guns – right on schedule – and Jan – well – she's the love of my life. I know I couldn't ask for better! How 'bout you? I hear we're going to be 'lantzmen,'" spoke Alex, slinging his arm over Matt's shoulder.

"'Lantzmen' – tell me about that?"

"Matt, it's kind of like when the blacks talk to each other – like 'Yo, bro' – or 'brother' – like from the same heritage, or blood brother."

"Sounds good to me, Alex! You know, since I've known your grandmother, I've become enamored, for lack of a better word, of her faith – your faith – this Judaism. Seems to answer a lot of questions for me about this mystique we call life."

"And *after* life, too, Matt? Does it hold some answers for you on that score, as well?"

"Yes, actually it does," Matt answered Alex, in a contemplative manner, staring off into space.

Alex waited, hoping Matt would bring up Nana's condition. But he was evading it, skirting it – so Alex let it be.

"Is your conversion to Judaism your gift to Nana?" Alex asked.

"I hadn't thought of it in quite those terms. But I suppose you might call it that. Yet, it's not the only reason," Matt answered softly.

"What do you make of Stephen Sohlberg? Do you and he hit it off all right?"

"Alex, I don't know really. At times Stephen does not appear well-disposed toward me. There's a degree of umbrage which takes place from time to time. He'll acknowledge my presence in a half-hearted manner, yet in his own kind of affable style."

"Stephen has always had a plaintive quality to his nature," Alex reflected. "Perhaps it's just more prominent now, with Sylvia's illness and all. And to be perfectly honest, Matt, I think he finds it difficult to broach the subject of you and Bess."

"No, I didn't mean in that regard. We seldom, if ever, even mention Bess' name."

"You may mistake Stephen's imperiousness for a pensive trait he has always possessed," Alex said amicably, but purposefully. "Matt, do you know that Stephen and Nana go way back? Theirs is a most unusual alliance – call it friendship – admiration. Borders on even more than mutual respect. It's difficult to explain, actually."

"Look, Alex, your grandmother told me before we were married. But I wasn't sure *you* knew the whole story. How did you come to know?"

"Oh, everyone in the family and all of Nana's closest friends, practically the whole community has known. Possibly Sylvia Sohlberg is the only one who hasn't figured it out! It didn't take a genius to understand the unusual closeness these two held for one another. And before you came along, Matt, Nana relied heavily on Stephen to get her through some very dark days. There was my grandfather's illness and his death and then the mourning process. I suppose in a way, Stephen may have some ambivalence toward you, Matt. From the time you and Nana fell in love, plus these past sixteen years of your marriage, she has had very little occasion to seek out Stephen. You see, he needed her as much as she needed him."

There was a deafening silence before Matthew spoke. "Oh. I'd really never thought about it in quite that way."

Alex quickly realized Matthew's discomfort with discussing Nana and Stephen's past relationship, so he changed the subject rather abruptly.

"Did you know, Matt, that we may use a Sukkah for our wedding in the fall? It's sort of like a chupah – only outside. What do you think?"

"Alex, to tell the truth, Stephen and I haven't gotten into the holidays all that much. But it sounds like a fine idea. I know your grandmother will be pleased. I built a Sukkah for her when we first met. I recall how specifically she explained that it was to have three sides, be open at the top so that one could see the light of day or the stars by night, and be big enough to fit your family and friends comfortably. And each year I've built a new and different style Sukkah," Matthew said wistfully.

Alex reflected for a moment on his past teachings and how much his grandmother loved this particular holiday. "I think I slept in a few of those Sukkahs of yours, Matt, in a sleeping bag! Nana would come outside every so often to check on me – and I'd pretend I was sleeping! When I was around twelve or thirteen, I even had a sleepover in one and when the rain came, we all rushed into Carlisle Way to dry off!"

"Yes, I remember that! And you wanted to eat all your meals out there for the entire week of Sukkot, and Bess let you!"

"I think the symbolism of Sukkot would be an interesting parallel with the marital vows," Alex said thoughtfully. "I can think back now to Nana's explanation about the true meaning of Sukkot. It went something like, 'Everything we have or own is transient. Like the Sukkah, no home is permanent or lasting. The only permanency we have is our individual spirituality – and our capacity to give and receive love and friendship. That's why a Sukkah is not a permanent structure. It was not intended to be. And so we build one anew each year!' Nana used to say, 'Alex, even Carlisle Way could be gone one day, but we would still retain our ability to be a friend or to love.'"

"And since it's a blessing – a 'mitzvot' I think you call it – to have several generations at your table in the Sukkah, this would fit nicely into the wedding theme," Matt added confidently.

"The only problem, Matt, is the size of our family and the number of friends we want to have."

"Alex, leave it to me. It'll be my pleasure to work out the details!"

Changing the subject, Matthew inquired with his innocent grin, "Knowing you, you aren't entering into this marriage lightly. Has your commitment to Jan passed the 'Friedman Test?'"

"It most certainly has! The very first thing Nana asked me when we announced our engagement was, 'Do you both pass the Friedman test?' Which is, of course, would I walk through fire and over hot coals for her, and would she do the same for me? The answer on both sides was quickly and positively in the affirmative! Nana and I chuckled over the criteria – and how she said she knew what my answer was before I gave it. She said it was like a family tradition – her own father asking her the same question when she announced her engagement to David Cantin!"

OUT OF MY peripheral vision, I saw Stephen Sohlberg kiss Nana on the cheek, saying his goodbyes. As he walked toward Matthew and me, he self-consciously smoothed his hair, what little he had, and adjusted his glasses. While Stephen's lenses were thicker and he was somewhat stodgier and bulkier in the middle, there was little change in his professorial appearance from the early days when I would see him at Carlisle Way. I knew that my grandfather, David Cantin, and he had been friends since their med school days. And that Stephen and his wife, Sylvia, and Nana and my grandfather had lived near one another in makeshift trailer apartments up on "The Hill" as they still call that section of married medical students at the University. As irony will have it, Jan and I will be living there come fall!

Stephen began as an internist and had a fine reputation in Loudonville as a diagnostician. But after ten or so years as a practicing physician, he went back to med school to study psychiatry. I was acutely aware, even as a young boy, of the special bond of friendship he had with Nana, and I recall being a bit jealous of him when he was at Carlisle Way, for Nana's eyes were averted from me – and focused on Stephen Sohlberg, no matter how much she tried to have it otherwise... This was especially true at the time of David Cantin's last years on earth and immediately after his death.

"Alex," called out Stephen, "I'm late for rounds, but

I'll try and catch up with you tomorrow. Want to hear the latest about you, Jan, med school – everything! Will you be here for a few days?"

I assured him I would and he waved as he stuck his head out the window of his car, revving up the engine of his old red Mercedes.

Matthew looked on and I could read him. He was wondering if it would befall Stephen or himself to break the news of Nana's illness and her impending mortality.

CHAPTER EIGHT

Chincoteague

*B*ESS, DO WE HAVE any more of those mustard and mayo packets?" Matthew called up to her as she was dressing for their outing. It was to be a "dry run," Stephen had said. They would only be going through the motions of the immersion – the "mikveh," Stephen had called it. "You know, Matt, get the lay of the land – and the water, too!" he had said.

"Mr. Matt," Maggie called out, "I be down there in a New York minute!" Maggie had adopted this expression from Bess many years back. "And I be showin' you where we done moved all that stuff!"

The special bathing suit, hand-sewn for Bess in Richmond, had been lying in a box for several weeks. Since the surgery she had needed a high-neck suit, with high-cut underarm coverage as well.

As Matthew reached up for the picnic plates, his eyes caught sight of Stephen's old red Mercedes, which Stephen had admitted to Matt he "had lusted after" for ages. Sylvia Sohlberg had a whole host of objections and often ran a disquieting commentary about the ills of convertibles, the color red and why Jews should never buy anything made in Germany!

Maggie, with her strong yet gentle hands, guided Bess' prosthesis into the bathing suit; to that part of her that had been taken away. Up 'til now, Bess had resisted Maggie's attentiveness and Matthew's offers of assistance. But now, Bess' feisty independence had given way to pragmatism.

"I declare, Miss Bess, this color is so becomin' to you! It goes with your hair and all. I been knowing you since you was a young bride. Luke, may God rest his soul, and me, we both talkin' bout you. It didn't matter no how how old you got or how you was fixin' your hair. You always one good-lookin' woman! Even now, what with you being sick and all, you still look better than most of them thin-lipped, scrawny white women you done worked with at them polling places!"

Bess' eyes were brimming over again. Although she was not one to indulge in sentimentality, Bess' attachment and deep affection for Maggie spilled out all at once.

"Oh, Maggie, my dear, sweet Maggie!" Bess reached out and took Maggie's hands in hers and kissed them. First she chose the dark side; then turning them over slowly, the pinkish, cracked, and work-worn parts as well.

It was the first time that Bess had confronted her illness with Maggie. With her eyes averting Bess' for the moment, Maggie held Bess in the kind of tight hug she generally reserved for the Cantin children and grandchildren.

"Promise we won't go on pretending that nothing is wrong, Maggie! Promise me, please! I can't talk with Matthew. He can hardly look at me without appearing like a lost child! I need you, dear Maggie, to let me be myself. I want to curse sometimes – scream – even cry! I have a right, don't I?"

Maggie let Bess go while still holding her gently by the shoulders. "You know, Miss Bess, you can talk to me any which way you want. If it makes you feel better, you can take a swing at me, child – you know that, don't you girl?"

"If death is a part of life, Maggie, then I must learn to embrace it! Can you help me do that, Maggie?"

"My peoples, we knows how to celebrate death all right! Why, sometimes, we even plays jazz on the way to that final resting place – when your time is a'comin'!"

Bess felt like a burden had been lifted off her back. Now she could talk openly and honestly with her new confidante. Even dear Stephen, with whom she had always confided, simply couldn't or perhaps wasn't able yet, to move away from his own denial of Bess' 'comin' of her time,' as Maggie phrased it.

Attempting to mask the pallor of her face, Bess pinched her cheeks as she descended the staircase. She could hear Matthew and Stephen in the kitchen, fixing "a short one for the road" – a little Jack Daniels with a slice of orange over ice, Matt's concoction of an Eastern Sour which was a holdover from his big city days.

Bess was wearing Matt's favorite color blue – the new bathing suit with its matching blouse and shorts, which she used this day as a cover-up. Seeing the two most important men in her life with their heads together, smiling and jostling over one man's satirical innuendo to another, gave Bess a warm and contented feeling. As she walked toward them – with a rather satisfied look, for Bess knew she had been blessed in having their love and devotion over the years – they both looked up at once.

"Ah, lovely lady of ours, resplendent in blue!" Stephen commented. In the old days, which he referred to as that time in their lives when all was "BMH" – Before

Matthew Held or various machinations on that theme – Stephen might have said, "Ah, lovely lady of mine!" But of course, that was only when he and Bess spoke privately.

Matthew rose to greet her, with outstretched arms – the same reaching out that Bess could always count on. "Bess, your hair braided like that with the ribbon all woven-in, why, it's perfect for our lunch by the Bay!" Placing his strong arm around her delicate waist, they walked together to where Maggie was finishing up the picnic lunch.

"I love what you've done with Miss Bess' hair, Maggie!" Matthew exclaimed.

"Thank you, Mr. Matt. Why I luvs to fool with that child's hair! You been knowin' that!" Maggie was fully aware that Bess' hair was becoming thinner each day from the chemo. Soon, she realized, Bess would be wearing a wig.

The onlooker Stephen, watching this vignette with a smile all too strained, pretended along with the others that all was well with this happy group. No one hated pretense more than Stephen Sohlberg. For once, he was unable to entertain a conversation that would alleviate his own discomfort and perhaps that of the others.

"Tell me, Stephen," piped up Matt, breaking the awkward silence, "how is this dress rehearsal for my 'rite of passage' going over with the powers that be? How do they really feel about a mikveh in the Chesapeake Bay? I get the sense we may be rockin' the boat!"

"It is said, my dear friend Matthew Held, that controversy swarms around even a handful of our brethren like bees to honey! Our most venerated committee of elders – the lay leaders of our synagogue and the 'bet din' – that triumvirate from Richmond, i.e., the rabbinical council – all agreed on our plan. Your high marks on

92

the written exam and your earnest study of Judaism have stood us in good stead. So when the 'hatafat dam brit' – the symbolic circumcision is over with..."

"Whoops – don't remind me!" said Matthew, looking downward. "This little guy is gonna go through some hellish moments, but I'll be intact, old man, don't you worry!" Matthew and Bess exchanged knowing looks for a brief moment.

"So this mikveh or tevilah, the immersion into the Chesapeake Bay, Matt, will be the second-to-last step in your becoming a Jew. Bess and I thought it might be a good idea, just the three of us, to go over the prayers and the rest of the immersion ritual. Besides, it's a beautiful day to float around in the Bay – eat some of Maggie's famous chicken salad sandwiches, make sand castles and even hold hands with Bess! You on?"

Blushing a bit, Bess spoke haltingly, letting her gaze linger a second or two upon Matthew and Stephen, attempting to gauge their reaction. They had been hovering over her of late, knowing full well of her uneasy grasp on life. Bess felt it was *she* who bore the burden of trying to cheer *them* up.

"On the way to Chincoteague," Bess said, with her vulnerability showing, "let's stop at Thymes' Gardens. Jan and Alex are coming in next week so we can get the wedding plans finalized. I want to check out their pottery and new plants. Oh – let's stop at the B&B Market to pick up some produce, too. Jan and I are coming up with some unusual decorations. Okay with you guys? We can do it on the way there or on the way home."

Matt knew the Old Thymes' Gardens was Bess' favorite greenery. But he also knew how tiring an afternoon at the beach would be for her, even with an umbrella, chair, hat and sunscreen. Suppressing his newly acquired patriarchal role, he quipped with Stephen and Bess about how he wanted to celebrate his "soon-to-be Jewishhood" by taking them all to Waterman's on the way home.

"That's a great idea, Matt. Let's stop at Thymes' on the way to Chincoteague and do the seafood dinner thing on the way back. Bess, you all right with that?" asked Stephen.

Bess squeezed herself in between Stephen and Matthew, sliding her arms, one across Matt's shoulders, the other around Stephen's. "Maggie," she trumpeted, "You may take the rest of the day and evening off. These two fine gentlemen are taking me to dinner!"

"Well, bless your hearts! We got a meetin' at church and a big supper tonight, too. I'm bringing Miss Bess' noodle puddin' – her famous 'koogel' she done taught me to make the first year I comes here. Right, Miss Bess?"

"And now Maggie, you make it better than I do!" Bess said smilingly.

"Mr. Matt. Don't you let Miss Bess get chilled none – ya hear with them bay breezes a sudden-like comin' up? I done laid out Miss Bess' sweatsuit, the one with the hood, and in case you need some blankets, I got them ready, too. You gots the chairs and umbrella in the trunk, Mr. Matt – and the sunscreen?"

"Ah Maggie, you're always a step or two ahead of me! Have a fine day. And when you're in church, put in a good word for me, will you?"

"You knows I does anyway, Mr. Matt, without you even askin'! Dr. Steve, I can't think of anything good to say 'bout you, but I'll ask the good Lord to watch over you anyway!" Maggie winked at Bess.

"Hey, what about me? What am I – chopped liver?" Bess beseeched Maggie.

"You iz in my prayers everyday! Now all of you – gets out of my kitchen! Play me some blues, Dr. Steve, and a little jazz, too. I luvs the way you play that piano," Maggie said as she turned back to her work while the rest obediently walked toward the den where the piano stood by the open window. Stephen was the last to leave the kitchen. As he passed by Maggie, he grabbed her girth in a dance hold. "I'll play the blues for you, dear old Maggie Williams, if you promise to sing me some soul music afterwards. We got a deal?"

As the others were out of earshot, Stephen abruptly stopped dancing with Maggie. Looking her boldly in the eye, and speaking quietly so only she could hear him, he lay bare what was in his heart. "We could all use a few hallelujahs around here, Maggie!"

"God knows we do, Dr. Steve! God knows!"

DURING THE RIDE toward the Assateague Channel and Chincoteague Island, Bess was extremely quiet. She closed her eyes and, placing her head on Matthew's arm, she listened to the "man-talk." The joy of hearing the male voice, with its rich baritone, seemed to Bess almost a sensual sound. Bess had once said, "A man's way of speaking has a mysterious power all its own."

Attempting to bring closure to an earlier discussion with Stephen regarding Matthew's religious background in the early years of his life, Matthew began musing about the chronology of his birth-religion as a Southern Baptist.

"I came rather reluctantly into my ancestral faith, but as a young adolescent growing up in a small southern community, there were social and fraternal benefits to be gained from one's conformity, regardless of conviction or core belief."

"Ah yes, ye olde Christian Fellowship concept,"

remarked Stephen.

"I suppose it was essential at that juncture of my life," echoed Matthew. "But with age, complacency took hold and I became more or less, over time, a non-believer."

"That is, until Bess, right? Why did you wait so many years, Matt, to become a Jew?" inquired Stephen.

"I can't readily answer that, Stephen. At first, I thought just living Jewishly with Bess would be enough to satisfy me. But I kept having more questions to be answered and you know the rest. Remember, living in LA, New York, Philly and the like, I had been thrown into close contact with artists and musicians of all colors and creeds and religions. Coming from my background, it was a three-way culture shock: ethnic, geographical and educational!"

"My God," Stephen blurted out, "were you at all intimidated?"

"Oh, yeah, at first I was. I was such a snob in those days! They thought me an intellectual snob so I was tolerated. It took me years to be conversant with blacks on an equal basis and with others from Asia or Third World countries – actually, any foreign land. My ancestors rolled over in their graves a few times, I guess."

"And women?" Stephen exhorted Matthew with his furrowed brow, "You have never appeared to me, in all the years I've known you, to have been a part of the 'Neanderthal' era! 'Egalitarian' was the first word I heard from Bess' lips to describe you!" Stephen smiled, as he tried to convey an openness with Matthew heretofore unknown.

Bess smiled inwardly as she harkened back to earlier discussions she and Matt had about the "humanity of women," as he termed it. She thought how even then

Matt's thinking was so far ahead of its time!

"Do you mind very much, Matthew, when I know something more about a given subject or I have another opinion?" she would inquire of him.

"Mind? Nonsense!" Matthew exclaimed. "I've known for years that most women have greater instincts and insights – even a depth of understanding – than men. Bess, you never laud the fact or overpower me with your knowledge. It's just out there – it merely is! You're never puffed up or are you a gloater! You know what I mean!"

"Of course, my darling," she would reply. "But the reason this type of discourse works for us is the fact that you possess no fragile or inflated ego!" Upon these discussions, silence would follow. They'd smile up at each other from their reading, attuned as they were to the rhythm that flowed between them in their friendship, as well as in their love.

"You didn't grow up here in Loudonville, Stephen. All was black and white, literally. A whole community – a mentality based on ignorance and fear. My God, Virginia's miscegenation law was still in effect until 1967."

Matthew continued, "I went from living in a township that would burn a cross on your front lawn for just walking a black girl home from school, to living in a dorm at VCU in Richmond, with Jews, blacks, and white folks from New York City – that den of iniquity! Of course, it wasn't until my apprenticeship in the fine arts materialized into jobs in the big cities that I had friends from all walks of life, including transvestites, gays, lesbians, bisexuals and the whole gamut of heterosexual deviations. My family was sure I was going to hell in a hand-basket, as my grandmother was fond of saying. And they thought all Jews had horns, according to David Cantin's father, who has regaled us with stories of growing up here. Why did you come here, Stephen, knowing what David and his family experienced?"

Stephen mused, "And Sylvia and her family, too. Well, I fought it at first, but you know Sylvia was so closely tied to her Dad's boat design and building business. She worked for years butting her head against the male bastion of this sphere of building. This was the only area, at least in those days, where she could make her mark. I could be a doctor anywhere, but she could not be a boat designer and builder anywhere, but on the Eastern Shore."

Bess had not seen Stephen in a few weeks and wondered if he was still contemplating retirement next year, as they had discussed when he last visited Carlisle Way.

"Stephen," she asked, "have you set a date for your retirement?"

"No, I haven't, but the sooner the better. Did you see the *New York Times* last month about the increasing number of requests for removing and storing the sperm of men who have just died?"

"I thought this procedure had been going on for a couple of decades," declared Bess.

"No, although you're right, technically speaking. The practice was still rare back then. But along with cloning and various forms of in-vitro, this dead-man-sperm issue is becoming more common. At The Center For Bioethics they're doing some studies. So far they've found an upswing in family requests for sperm in the past few years."

"Have any children been conceived with sperm posthumously retrieved?" inquired Bess.

"No, none that I know about. But look, we are getting into murky waters every time I turn around, that go far beyond the annals of medical procedures. There are moral, ethical, religious, and legal issues aplenty here. For starters, how do you resolve the ethics of taking sperm without the consent of the donor? I'm getting calls almost weekly from all over the country; mostly physicians who want to take sperm from dead men and wonder whether it's legal or ethical. We're all floundering in an area where the rules are uncertain."

"But what about the organ donation law?" asked Matt. "Doesn't this law allow next of kin the right to donate a dead person's body parts and decide on the recipient?"

Delaying his answer to Matthew to a degree, Stephen went on. "Most of my bioethicist colleagues would like to see a more coordinated national policy. We need some lines drawn in the sand. For one thing, what we have now is a 'show-me-the-money' mentality by individual doctors. In other words, if you can pay, you'll most likely get the service."

"I agree with you, Stephen," Bess ventured. "A policy that can change human relationships such as saving sperm from a dead man to impregnate a woman – like his wife, his girlfriend, his cousin, his aunt – I mean, just whom would the recipient have to be? I agree, we need strong governmental guidelines."

"Well," said Stephen, contemplating how far he could go with these laymen on this issue and other bioethical ones that stuck in his craw, "I think soon a man's sperm will be listed on the donor card, which will allow the man, in this case, to decide if and to whom his sperm will go when he dies. And look at this cloning business...."

"Stephen," broke in Matt, "didn't you tell me you were going to testify before the National Bio-Ethics Advisory Commission on the subject of cloning?"

"Yes, I just got back, Matt. So far we have a

moratorium on using federal funds for human cloning research and there is an ongoing committee that has to report to the President within ninety days whether this new technology should be even more tightly controlled. And we've also recommended that the cloning of a human being, no matter who pays for it, should be a criminal offense in the United States. Now what we need is for the Congress to give our conclusions the force of law. Cloning human beings is a hot-button issue. I think we'll be debating cloning well into the millennium. If future research shows cloning to be safer and the attitude of society in general changes, we've recommended that any legal ban be re-evaluated after three to five years. Some experts in the in-vitro fertilization field are really disappointed. They have testified that cloning might be the only chance for many infertile couples to have their own genetically related children."

"So, as they say, 'you're out of there,'" affirmed Bess.

"Yes, I've given notice. As soon as they find a replacement for me, I'll be leaving. I'm just not cut out to be a man of the nineties – at least that is, as a medical man. God knows what will transpire in bioethics in the year two-thousand and beyond! Truthfully folks, I'm weary of the open debate, and even more importantly, the inner one. What I want to do now is some writing, a little traveling and I think by way of adventure, I'll take up sailing. I'll find some new challenges – you know me! But not the gut-wrenching ones any longer. I don't have the stomach for it!"

"Ay, Stephen, my good man, may the wind be always at your back," Matthew remarked in his Irish brogue which served him well when he was at a loss for words.

Bess smiled knowingly as she realized how much Matthew and Stephen's friendship had progressed.

Stephen drove, as Bess said, like a bat out of hell, and even now she still found it necessary to gently prod him into slowing down.

"Remember the speed traps on 13 North?" she asked Stephen. "The state troopers would prefer nothing better than pulling over a car bearing northern plates. And at the same time, they would take great pleasure in giving a ticket to a guy who not only is a doctor, but who still enjoys a New Rochelle accent!"

"Henceforth, your ladyship, your wish shall be done!" Stephen said as he smiled and peered through his rearview mirror at Bess.

APPROACHING Chincoteague Island, Matthew's memories, vividly placed in his mind, could be summoned up as quickly and accurately as a sports telecaster's instant replay. The recall Matthew seemed to delight in the most, that brought him a chuckle or two, even when he was alone, was when Bess and he first became lovers. When their naked feet rubbed up against each others' for the first time, Bess felt the roughened skin of his soles and heels and asked how he had acquired such toughness. "Ah," she had said before he could explain, "now I know why the hot sand never seems to faze you!"

"As a kid," he told her, "growing up on the Eastern Shore, we had a kind of ritual on the first day of our summer vacation. We'd take off our shoes and wouldn't put them back on again 'til Sunday church and the first day of school. Beforehand, just to toughen up our feet more, we'd look for road construction, of which there was plenty, and proceed to walk and run on the gravel. It hurt, but it did the job! At that age – I guess we were about twelve or thirteen –" Matthew said laughingly, "it only served to prove we had very little going on

101

between our ears!"

"My dear one," he remembered her saying, "I have a special cream that Maggie makes up for me, for these gardening hands. I think a Bess Cantin foot-massage with Maggie's cream is in order here. It shall be done regularly before or after making love!"

"Let me see those feet of yours!" Matthew exhorted when she first broached the subject. He had risen up to press his lover's foot onto his palm. As he did so, he noted for the first time, the delicate toes, so evenly arranged in their contour. He had thought to himself, "even my love's feet are perfect! Are there no imperfections on the physical being of this woman?" He was to discover, in the ensuing months, birthmarks of various sizes and shapes in unusual places, to which he often referred to as Bess' "larger freckles" as he kissed each and every one.

Matthew, like Bess, loved to feel the wind and sun on his face. After making sure Bess' scarf was wrapped securely around her ears and neck, he too laid his head back on the leathery cushion of Stephen's car and began to let his thoughts linger over the experiences he had had as a boy growing up near Chincoteague. And then the special memories came to the fore – of the blissful days and nights spent with Bess, or with Bess and Alex, and on occasion, Bess, he, Alex and Amy.

The children, when small, were enchanted by the pony-penning that occurs annually in late July on Chincoteague Island. Crossing only at slack tide, when the high tide and the low tide come together, a herd of about one hundred and fifty wild ponies swim across Assateague Channel and are sold at auction.

Small, shaggy-coated, big bellied and squarely built, the Chincoteague ponies move at a slow and measured pace. These hardy animals are, by folklore, descended from horses that were shipwrecked or arrived with the pirates centuries ago. Amy was about six or seven years old and an avid fan of the Chincoteague pony when she began a scrapbook of her renderings of the ponies and their surroundings. At Carlisle Way, in the room reserved for Amy's overnight visits, are the memorabilia of their frequent trips to the Islands. Standing atop her bookcase, one can see a copy of her favorite childhood book: Marguerite Henry's *Misty of Chincoteague*.

Matthew believed that Alex's love of kayaking and his recent proficiency at windsurfing derived from the many vacations they spent exploring the abundant waters nearby.

Whenever Alex needed a "partner in crime," Matthew became the go-fer. He and Alex would laugh about Matt's desire to learn all these new sports with Alex – no matter Matt's advancing years. Alex realized early on that Matthew was the type of man to give his "best shot" to every challenge he took on. Sometimes he and Alex just hung loose. The boy was at that age when his own rhythms were in dominance, often contrasting to or unable to correspond to adult whims, wishes or rules. Bess kept to hiking and cycling along the wilderness trails and sometimes Matt and Alex would join up with her, after doing the day's share of male bonding.

They often stayed at The Refuge Inn, where Amy could visit with some of the ponies in the Inn's own pasture. There they were only a mile and a half from the Atlantic Ocean and could all rent bicycles to ride to the beach.

The fishing village of Chincoteague has a New England charm to it, even now, reflected Matthew, and always reminded him of the Capes, where he had vacationed during his Boston years. Chincoteague, in

Matthew's mind, was a land that time had forgotten. There was a tranquility about the place which he and Bess sought during the early years of their love affair and eventual marriage. They called Chincoteague and Assateague Islands their sanctuaries.

Bess loved the unbroken beach, with its rolling dunes, the level marshlands and the freshwater ponds. She believed that the islands contained the rarest stretch of wild seashore on the East coast. He and Bess never tired of roaming through the turn-of-the-century fishing villages. Matt was always amazed at how many people remembered him and asked as to the health and whereabouts of his kin.

Matthew reminded himself of the first time Alex ate an oyster at the annual Chincoteague Island Oyster Festival, held nearabout Columbus Day weekend. When Alex first spied the renowned Chincoteague oyster – all shimmery and jelly-like, sliding around in its own juice, resting in its shell – he said, "I may puke my guts out, Matt! That's a lame lookin' item there. I think I'll just have a hot dog instead." But later on, as Matt and Bess devoured their plates of raw oysters and were moving onward to the steamed and fried variations, Alex was to be seen sneaking a bit of a fried oyster sandwich which had rested on Bess' plate. Now he was hooked for life. He explained: "They just needed a little fixin' before they were edible, is all!"

On their last trip here when Bess was well, they stayed at Miss Molly's Inn, a bed-and-breakfast place in the grand old Victorian style, where they both looked forward, at the end of the afternoon's trek, to a traditional English afternoon tea with an Eastern Shore variety of a crumpet.

In 1962, when the Ash Wednesday storm devastated Chincoteague, and along with it, Matthew's family farm,

Matthew came home from Chicago to work alongside the local neighbors, helping to put the town back together.

As they passed familiar landmarks such as Temperance-ville, Thomas' Gardens (another of Bess' beloved greeneries) and the Country Goose, where they had always purchased their gifts for family and dear friends, Matthew inquired of Stephen as to just which beach area he had chosen for this momentous occasion.

"I talked to the Leonards. They asked for you, Matt. They offered to let us park there and we can walk to the beach from their place which is about a mile and a half. My plan is to drop off our stuff at the beach area – the chairs, blankets and picnic, with Bess – and then you and I can walk on down there or bike, if you want."

Matthew had brought with him, and actually wore under his khakis, the loose-fitting bathing suit made of porous material that Stephen had explained would allow Matthew to adhere, as much as possible, to the traditions of the tevilah. "One is really supposed to be completely unclothed as is done in the indoor pool-like mikveh that is usually adjacent to, or inside, the synagogue. We don't want to cause a riot on a public beach, Matt, thus the extra large trunks which I will ask you to hold out at about two inches on each side when you're immersed."

"I'm supposed to tread water while I hold *up* – I mean *out* – my suit, correct?"

"Yes, Matt. That's right. Bess, I'll move your chair and umbrella closer to the water so you can see and hear better," said Stephen, as he and Matt moved all the things to the water's edge on a part of the beach which was more secluded than the rest, almost like a cove.

Stephen held two copies of the prayer plus two head-coverings (the kippot). He tried to adjust one of the skullcaps on Matthew's full head of hair, by trying to adhere specially made clips strategically placed to allow the kippah from slipping. To do this, he had had to ask Matthew to sit on a chair because Matt was so tall. Instead of sitting, Matthew got on his knees at the foot of Bess' chair and asked her, "Will you bestow upon this adoring knight, his armor, my lady?"

Bess obliged. With her hands quaking, she slipped the skullcap onto Matthew's hair, using more than the usual number of clips, as Bess knew Matt was going to be immersed three times with his head completely submerged. Matt had used a waterproof marker to write the two prayers, one on each arm, because he knew he could not keep a hand-held paper from being drenched. He had balked at having to say the prayers in Hebrew. At one of their religious discussions, Matthew had explained, "Look, Stephen, I've never been real good at languages. I'm having a hell of a lot of trouble decoding the Hebrew. Would it be terribly irreligious of me to just say these two prayers in English?"

Stephen acknowledged that Matthew had been given a formidable task – to learn the prayers in Hebrew along with attempting to comprehend their relevancy; being able to understand the tenets of Judaism and absorb the history of the Jews; the holidays and the significance of the Sabbath – all in a matter of six months!

"I understand, Matt. It's okay, really," Stephen assured him. "Are you ready? At the real ceremony, the Rabbi from Salisbury is coming in. A colleague of mine will act as the second witness. I'll be the third."

Then there they were, Matthew and Stephen, striding exuberantly into the water. Treading water, Matthew said the first blessing aloud after the first submersion. "Blessed are you, Oh Lord, our God, ruler of the Universe, who has sanctified us by your commandments and commanded us concerning the ritual of immersion."

Following Stephen's countdown instructions, Matthew Held pulled out his swimsuit about two inches from his body at the waist and went under, head and all. A total immersion. "I've been mikvehed!" he thought to himself. As he came up for air, his eyes and Bess' fastened onto each other and he saw her pride in him.

Saying the second blessing, "Blessed are you, Oh Lord, our God, ruler of the Universe, who has granted us life, for sustaining us and for helping us to reach this day," Matt again pulled out his swimsuit two inches from each side and, letting the waves caress his body, he slid down under the foam that had crested atop the wave. (At the real ceremony, he would immerse himself a third time.) When he arose this time from underwater, he took a long lanky stride, and dripping wet, he plopped himself down onto the blanket next to Bess' chair. She wasn't at all worried about getting soaked or salted, for Bess Cantin knew Matthew's embrace could not be stopped. She hugged him with what little strength she possessed in her frail body. Only she knew of the elation Matthew was experiencing. For this moment was reflected in his peaceful smile which buoyed his spirit and hers on this day.

The kinship felt by Stephen, the teacher, the friend, the lover of Matthew's wife, was immediate and overwhelming. Although Stephen perceived the couple's need for privacy, his discerning awareness of why *he* was there bound him inextricably to them.

There was no time left for waiting, nor for humility or false pride. Resting on the sand next to Bess' chair, after Bess and Matthew had concluded their embrace, Stephen began to bury her feet in the sand.

"Why don't we build a castle for Bess?" he suggested,

as he nimbly gathered cups of water to moisten his section of sand. Bess peered down through her darkened lenses and commiserated, "From this communion we have all three become fused," and she arose from her queenly throne to help them build this homage.

IT WAS THAT TIME of the evening when the sun darkened, and not too far in the distance one could detect the formation of a small puff of white, soon to be referred to as moon.

Stephen put the top up on the convertible; he knew the night air would cause too much of a chill for Bess, even with her hooded jacket.

"Bess," suggested Matthew, "why don't you sit up front with Stephen? I think it will be less breezy in the front."

Bess nodded her head and moved in closer to Stephen. She touched Stephen's hand, and left it lying on top of his for several minutes. He did not withdraw it. And for both of them, the touching still held the magic: the quickened heartbeat, the stillness in their desire to be at peace with one another, and the pure enjoyment of seeing each other's breath evaporate into the same air which both were breathing at that given moment.

As Stephen's hands steered them through the night, Marian McPartland was playing the piano on the local public broadcasting station, mixing her special blend of blues and jazz, which became the backdrop for the three of them to luxuriate in the silence of their thoughts.

STEPHEN WAS REMINDED of their attempt, he and Bess, at a weekend away together in Chincoteague for the annual pony penning. It had been about six or seven months after David had passed away and before the advent of Matthew Held. Sylvia Sohlberg had been attending a boat show at Annapolis, and the boys were all out of the house by then. Bess and Stephen had reserved adjoining rooms at the Refuge Motor Inn, and the anticipation of that weekend alone with Bess, of hopefully making love to her at long last, made Stephen feel as if he were twenty-one again! But the day before they were to leave, Bess phoned him up.

"Stephen," she had begun hesitantly, "Alex is going through a particularly rough time right now. As a thirteen-year-old teenager, with his hormones raging, on top of dealing with that, his parents, Ann and Lem, are on the brink of divorce. And of course, their dirty linen is hung out to dry, even in front of their children! This is the only weekend they have been able to plan a private meeting between themselves and to also have a therapy session. Let's take Alex with us, Stephen, could we? Can it be the three of us?"

There was a long period of silence. Stephen recalled that space of time. He, seldom at a loss of words, finally answered, "Of course, Bess. I know that's the right thing to do. Yes, Sure. We'll have fun." Bess could sense Stephen's disappointment. It was apparent in his voice. He had never been adept at camouflaging his innermost feelings.

And so on the next day, they all left together. After a day of swimming in the ocean and watching the ponies swim across the Assateague Channel to Chincoteague Island, they ate a hearty dinner and retired early.

After Alex had seemingly fallen asleep, Bess put on her robe and came out onto the balcony of their room. Stephen had not completely given up smoking, so Bess could make out the burning ash of his cigarette on the adjacent balcony.

He approached her, climbing over the railing that separated their rooms. He took her in his arms and kissed her with all the passion that he had saved for her these many years. And she, Bess Cantin, responded in kind. He loosened the sash of her robe and slid the sleeves gently away from her body. Stephen savored the moment – the mystery of what might have been or what might be – the wonder of the almost.

In all the time that Stephen Sohlberg had loved Bess Cantin (or Bess Friedman when they first met in College), he had hardly touched her. They had kissed passionately, once, in his study. And in a few of the many therapy sessions, when they also spoke of their longing for one another, they had allowed themselves a small measure of intimacy: Bess would place her head on Stephen's shoulder and he would lovingly stroke her hair.

"Bess, Bess," Stephen had implored her, "our time together on this planet is quickly vanishing! All the while, when David was ill and then when he died, you and I became as close as one. Is there now a place for me in your life? My lovely friend, my confidante, I want to be your husband! I am planning on asking Sylvia for a divorce. We haven't lived as man and wife for a long time," Stephen said, somewhat emboldened.

"Stephen, how can you say you will divorce Sylvia? She isn't well, darling, you know that, although you never talk about it. You once said to me, when I spoke of leaving David, something like: 'One cannot gain personal happiness at the expense of another.' Stephen, you have to be there for her! Your leaving would only exacerbate her condition. And knowing you as I do, you couldn't live with yourself! The fabric of *our* marriage, too, would be torn apart!"

"Bess, did you ever want me as your lover?"

"I thought we've been lovers all these years!"

"Bess, you know what I'm saying. Did you ever want

me physically?"

"I wanted you desperately all the years you counseled me, even in the beginning, at your lectures. Your voice had a way of mesmerizing me. It was like an aphrodisiac – holding me captive. I used to fantasize sleeping with you. But you were so damn honorable in those days, so I never pursued it. But want you I did! I even used to dream of lying in your arms and I'd be in a cold sweat upon awakening. In the long run, Stephen, it comes down to the simple fact that I never go where I sense I'm not wanted."

"Bess, believe me, you were wanted! I simply didn't know how to handle it."

"Stephen, may I confess something to you?"

"Confess, confess away, dear lady! Wait, I shall draw the curtain closed – look – I'm in my booth!"

"Be serious, please, Stephen. After your lectures or our therapy sessions my eyes would well up, I was so consumed in my desire for you. And when I played a tape of Rachmaninoff's Second Concerto while driving home from being with you, I wept."

"Oh, Bess, darling."

"And now, one more confession. Maybe it was to distract me from thinking of what was going wrong with David, or with David and me – the mind works in such strange ways. I'd dream up ways of seducing you!"

"Seduce, seduce, fair one!"

"I'll tell you just one scenario. I had just bought an emerald green taffeta raincoat. And one of the days we were to meet at your office, I was planning to wear it without anything under it! Do you believe me capable of such a thing? Do you understand now what desire for you I held? Stephen, look at me, please. Please don't be forlorn We will always be intimates of a kind."

111

Bess took Stephen's thick glasses off and touched his face and kissed him hard. It was only when she turned aside to cover her mouth as a sneeze was about to erupt, that her peripheral vision allowed her to see Alex sitting up in his bed, watching them.

At first, Alex's face wore a puzzled expression, but because he was accustomed to seeing Stephen at Carlisle Way, even when David was living, teaching Bess the latest dance step while holding her close, putting his arm around her at the piano when they played together, he merely waved to them, offering up his endearing smile. He mouthed the words, "I can't sleep," as he turned on the bedside light and began to read his science fiction novel. Still, Bess raised up the back of her robe and tied the sash, leaning her body into Stephen's to imply that all was right.

When Bess told him that Alex had seen them kiss, Stephen whispered to her, "Come here, you seductress!" He placed his arm tightly around her shoulders, allowing her head to rest upon his arm, and stroked her hair the way he had done so many times in his study.

Although it pained Stephen to recall that day, that night, in such detail, he knew it was necessary. He had been chastened and humbled, penitent, with self-reproach. But now that Bess was ill, he would be able to transcend the poetic poignancy of their relationship in order that he might subscribe to the inevitable bereavement almost upon him. His faith would bring him solace. He and Matthew together, fending off the demons of loss.

As Stephen's car came to a stop in the driveway of Carlisle Way, Matthew asked him to escort Bess into the house, while he went out back to put the pots and plants on the rear porch. As Bess opened the door with her key, she looked long and hard at Stephen. She quietly said, "I'll be needing Brahms very soon now, Stephen. Will you play for me? My own private concert?"

Stephen smiled and nodded yes, but was unable to utter a word, knowing the syllables he wanted to form would take hold of his throat and leave him speechless.

$\mathcal{M}$y *beloved speaks and says to me:*
Arise, my love, my fair one, and come away.
For lo, the winter is past, the rain is over and gone.
The flowers appear on the earth, the time of
singing has come, and the voice of the turtledove
is heard in our land....

From *Song of Songs* as transcribed in
the standard text of the wedding service,
presented in the Rabbinical Assembly Manual

CHAPTER NINE

Matthew, Stephen and Margaret "Maggie" Williams

ALTHOUGH NOW "professor emeritus," Stephen Sohlberg still lectured extensively in the field of medical/legal ethics. He had cut back on his psychiatric practice upon reaching his seventieth birthday, yet still maintained an office within the confines of the medical school.

It was here, in Stephen's rather small, spartan quarters, that Matthew came for most of his weekly conversion sessions. The inner door to Stephen's office was closed. Matthew sat down in the outer room awaiting Stephen's usual congenial greeting. It had been Stephen's idea, his sense of conviviality, explained Bess, to have lunch with Matthew while holding forth in their Judaic discourse on conversion. Stephen had inquired of Matthew's vegetarian commitment and had managed to have delivered to his office each week something imaginative to please Matthew's palate and his dietary regimen.

Perhaps it was the rarefied air of academia, but Matthew's thoughts, no matter how earnestly he attempted to avert them, ruminated toward remembering that it was in these very rooms that Bess Cantin and Stephen

Sohlberg lay bare the dissension, the discord which plagued their respective marriages. It was here, Matthew painfully realized, where Bess and Stephen became inextricably bound in their search for tranquility; in their shared vision of that which transcends the pain and beauty of love unfulfilled.

The hushed tones, bespeaking the love between Bess and Stephen, implying their spiritual affinity, one for the other, were lurking there for Matthew each time he stood amongst the book-lined walls, reading the certificates bearing witness to Dr. Stephen Sohlberg's brilliance.

It was almost as if he had been privileged to be a part of their sessions. Like a voyeur, Matthew pictured them holding hands, aching with longing to touch one another, while his own shadowy figure looked on.

The poignancy these thoughts brought on, knowing full well that Bess had belonged to Stephen, in heart and soul, before he had come along, was sometimes overwhelming. Should he, he pondered, ever bring himself to acknowledge this pain, this remembering, to Stephen's ears? Probably not to do so was best for now, thought Matthew, at least until at such time, if ever, he and Stephen would become close friends.

For now, Matthew felt comfortable with their relationship. He assured himself that Stephen no longer merely tolerated him. He had earned Stephen's respect for the conscientious way in which he was studying Judaism. Matthew Held was aware that at the very least, Stephen Sohlberg placed value upon him because Bess Cantin did.

Stephen opened his inner-office door. Behind him, a rather meek-looking young man appeared to be groping with papers and pens, books and folders.

"Chris, keep up the good work. I'll see you next month – same time."

Toward Matthew, and Chris' back, he gave his raised-eyebrow-look which meant Chris must be either a lost cause or someone who Stephen was bringing along simply because he possessed other gifts worthy of mitigating a lack of scholarly acumen.

"The boy lacks confidence," he told Matthew. "But he has promise."

"I see you're still advising. How many students this year?" inquired Matthew.

"Only five. Down from ten last year. I'm cutting back – slowing down. Who knows, I may even retire completely next year," Stephen added almost as an afterthought.

"Shall we eat first? I'm famished," remarked Stephen. In fact, let's eat and talk. I've got a tight schedule today."

"That'd be fine. Except I feel embarrassed to be bringing up the Holocaust while we're eating. Poor form. I mean it. Seems almost sacrilegious!" Matthew exclaimed.

"No problem for me, Matt. Listen, don't worry if we aren't able to touch upon all the stuff I gave you to read last week. It was an awful lot to absorb."

"Hmmm. Well, here goes. How could something as horrific as the Holocaust have occurred to 'The Chosen People?'" Matthew asked.

"Ah, yes, the inevitable question. If there is a God of the Jews, how could this have happened? Matt, I once attended a symposium of Holocaust survivors. One of them raised the question, '*Where was God?*' Another survivor answered him. 'It was not God who was absent, but *man*. The question should be '*WHERE WAS MAN?*' This philosophy is based on the Jewish teachng that God created man and gave him free will. When we use that free will and commit evil deeds, then *we* are responsible."

Matthew seemed to agree, and said, "Here, in one

of the books you loaned me – the one by Pinchas Peli on interpreting the Torah, I like this part – and I believe it relates to what you're talking about: 'Goodness is not inherited, but must be acquired in a lifetime of decision-making. Every day, every moment, a person must decide between good and evil. The human is born in his aloneness with the capacity to choose between good and evil.'"

"Yes, Peli. One of my favorite authors. The way I see it, Matt, the Holocaust is a classic example of man's inhumanity to man. Rabbi Kushner's book – that's in the pile of books I loaned you, *When Bad Things Happen To Good People* – addresses this question in depth. Kushner believes, along with many Jewish scholars, that, for example, if a plane falls out of the sky or if a baby is born with a birth defect – what do we say? That this is God's punishment for a sin which we committed knowingly or unknowingly? Why could it not be a mechanical problem with the plane or miscalculation or ineptitude by the pilot? And in the case of the child – could it not simply be a genetic abnormality? Why must we hold God accountable for all of life's tragedies – all the ills of the world? I for one go along with Kushner."

Matthew chimed in, "I think I see what you're saying. For instance, in the two areas you just talked about – if we were more diligent about maintaining our planes and training our pilots, maybe that plane wouldn't have fallen out of the sky. And if we prioritize our national budget – perhaps with more money allotted for genetic research and prenatal care – we might be able to cut down on birth defects. Man's responsibility to his fellow man!"

"Right, Matt. Look, God gave us a heart, a mind and a soul. And we are the only species he trusted with a conscience! So, it's up to us, to each individual, to do what we will with these gifts God bestowed upon us."

"Speaking about the era of the Holocaust," Matthew added haltingly, "I've been reading that converts didn't fare very well. Many were gassed in the concentration camps along with those who were Jewish-born. Many were tortured for having selected Judaism over their original religion."

"You want to stop now, Matt, before it's too late?"

"If I didn't know your sense of humor by now, I'd be offended!" Matt retorted, rather defiantly, yet maintaining his equanimity as always.

"I guess this is as good a time as any to remind you, to *dissuade* you, as a matter of fact, Matthew Held, from becoming a Jew! This is part of my duty as your mentor in the conversion process. Because, let's face it, the Jewish people have been defiled and discriminated against since the beginning of time. I'm sure you're aware of this by now, having lived Jewishly, and with a Jewish woman such as Bess these many years.

"There still remains an attitude toward Jews that lingers in many places. How about right here – in Loudonville, on the Eastern Shore of Virginia? I think we can rightly say that anti-Semitism still festers.

"Matt, you're not just joining a church, but a way of life. We are a people against whom prejudice is still evident. You should be reminded – warned may be a more accurate word – that you are becoming a minority!"

Stephen went on. "In fact, let me see. In one of the texts concerning conversion, it says, 'One who is contemplating conversion to Judaism should be asked, 'Do you know that this nation is downtrodden more than all other nations?'"

"Let's move on," Matthew replied. "I think you know of my commitment, Stephen."

"Do you mind telling me, Matt, one more time, why

119

you want to become Jewish? Why now?"

"Well, you know of her trip to Europe with her Grandfather after the war, and you already know so well that Judaism has always been such a strong part of Bess' life. So, maybe becoming a Jew is my way of trying to hold on to her. I know she's dying, Stephen, even though we don't speak of it."

Stephen turned his swivel chair toward the window, and looked out over the campus, barely acknowledging Matthew. He heard his every word.

Matthew continued, "There is an attitude of transcendence within Judaism that I see about facing the death of a loved one. I want to embrace Bess' values; to emulate her. Being Jewish, I will be closer to her when I can no longer touch her. By my being Jewish, I will help to keep her soul alive. I think – no, I don't think – I *know* that my Jewish faith will give meaning and expression to my sorrow.

"The whole process of Jewish mourning is so sensitive – such an intense experience. There is nothing cold or abstract about it. The week of 'shivah' – the seven days – the gathering-in of family and friends – then the thirty days – the 'sheloshim.' For a year, the year of mourning, I, if I'm Jewish, can be a part of the morning and evening prayer service; be counted upon as one of the ten required to pray together. I feel, when I'm in my seat at the chapel at the Hillel House – I don't know – I feel buffeted – comforted by the chanting and the words of meditation – the prayers. It's a warm place to be, and I will need that warmth – especially without Bess."

Stephen quietly replied, "Matthew, please don't look away. I've never doubted your sincerity. I have to ask and re-ask – it's part of my job. Forgive me for having to put you through this. I won't have to ask again. That's a promise."

"Thank you, Stephen. What's next on the agenda?"

"'Sincere proselytes are considered close to God,' so it says here in the text of laws concerning proselytes or the would-be convert. Let me read this to you. 'Had the Israelites not witnessed the thunder, lightning, quaking mountains, and sounding of trumpets atop Mount Sinai, they would *not* have accepted the Torah. But the proselyte, who saw *not* one of these things, came and surrendered himself to the Holy One, blessed be He, and took the yoke of heaven upon himself. *Can anyone be dearer to God than this man?*'"

"Not bad, Stephen, I'll take it!"

"Let me see your Peli book a minute, will you Matt? I recall something about how Abraham was led to discover the land which is now known as Israel.

"Here it is. 'When Abraham was searching for the land which was later to be known as Israel, God did not tell Abraham from the start which land he was to go to. Abraham realized his destination upon seeing inhabitants engaged in weeding and hoeing at the proper season. And Abraham exclaimed, 'Would that my portion might be in *this* country!' 'Said the Holy One, blessed be He, to him (Genesis 15:18). Unto thy seed have I given THIS land.'

"You see, Matt, ever since then, 'this Land' has remained for the people of Israel tied-in with equal intensity to both the spiritual and the earthly dimensions. Do you mind if I recite this at your conversion ceremony? It speaks to who you are, Matt, your love of the land and your spirituality, as well."

"I'd be honored to have you read that section or anything you deem appropriate, Stephen. You do me honor. "

"Have you and Bess talked about a Hebrew name?"

121

"Yes. It is to be 'Matityahu ben Avraham Avinu' – Matthew, son of our father, Abraham!'"

"Now, that's a handle! Most impressive!"

"Got a nice ring to it," Matthew responded proudly, and then went on, "Stephen, can we talk about this *Talmud* and *Torah*? What exactly are they, in your view?"

"The Talmud and the Torah are the basic tenets of Judaism. The Talmud – the books of the Talmud – are a sort of repository of Jewish laws pertaining to man's daily dilemma of decision-making in his living and working with others, and in his relationship with the Almighty.

"To my mind, Torah in reality is the Jewish bible. And the purpose of the laws of the Torah is to refine man. Put another way, Torah is the essence of life and how to live it. It – the Torah, that is – is the first five books of Scripture. Rabbinical scholars say, 'keep turning to the Torah again and again, because everything is in it.'

"To define Torah even more, the great rule or the all-inclusive principle, or if you wish, the totality of the entire Torah, is in one line, – 'love your neighbor as yourself.'"

Stephen spoke proudly. "I rather like this paragraph that I've highlighted. 'All human beings, each of them are created in the likeness of God. Love of others is not to be dependent on love of oneself, but on the fact of each individual's God-given precious uniqueness.'

"Altruistic love is an invention of Torah, says Peli. The reason for loving our fellow human being is not for the sake of being loved. It is because 'I am the Lord! God Himself is love.' (This is Peli's description). 'And humans,' he interprets the Torah here, 'deserve to be loved because they were created in His image;' because every other human being is *kamocha*, just like you. A person, not a number. An original, not a carbon copy!

"Here Peli goes on. 'Self-preservation, self-gratification, is the natural inclination of any living creature, humans included. Whoever heard of loving others' he says, 'for other than selfish reasons – until the Bible of the Hebrews came and put before us the command of non-utilitarian love: LOVE OF GOD, OF NEIGHBOR AND OF STRANGER?'"

"Can I see the book for a minute?" Matthew turned quickly to a page which he had previously marked. "Here, when he, Peli, talks about the Mishna, the ancient code of Jewish law, he elaborates – and this is by far my favorite part. 'Let other people's possessions be as precious to you as your own. As you would not want yours to be wasted, do not waste others'. Let others' dignity be as safeguarded as you wish yours to be. Do not violate other people's dignity, self-esteem or right to hold their own views.'"

"Matt, you've done your homework well! One last mention of Peli's interpretations of Torah – I'm especially fond of this section. 'The true test of this commandment about loving thy neighbor as thyself is in loving those who are *not* as good and lovable in one's eyes. Love your fellow human as yourself, as you accept yourself with all your faults and shortcomings, accepting others the same way.'"

"I guess that's the true test – the real challenge, isn't it?"

"I believe so, Matt."

Matthew paused. "You've done so much with your life, Stephen. I want to admit here and now to being in awe of you; have been since we first met. And now this faith of yours – it flows so naturally. I want to say something. I know this sounds a bit odd – but your faith fits you well! You wear it like a mantle!"

"Thank you, Matt. The sages are fond of saying that they have learned that it doesn't much matter whether a man does much or little, if only he directs his heart to heaven.

"Once, a long time ago, I had an admiring non-believer friend say to me, 'I wish that I had your faith so that I might lead a life like yours.' My answer, although not entirely an original, went something like, 'Lead my life and you *will* acquire my faith.' Another scholar explained, 'Even if one commits a good act out of an unworthy motive, he will, if he persists, come to be governed by a right motive.'"

Matthew joined in, "I found this quote from among the books you gave me. 'He whose wisdom exceeds his deeds, to what may he be compared? To a tree of many branches, but few roots which the wind can easily pluck up and overturn. But he whose deeds exceed his wisdom, to what may he be compared? To a tree of few branches but many roots which, even though the strongest wind blow upon it, will not be moved!'"

"You've accomplished a great deal in just a matter of months, Matt. We are way ahead of schedule!"

"I felt that time was of the essence. I wanted my conversion to take place before Bess ... you know what I'm saying."

"Yes, Matt. I know. I've been in touch with the 'bet din,' the rabbinical council, explaining the necessity of haste because of Bess' condition. I have also explained to the council how you and Bess feel about the Bay, and they have agreed that you may have the immersion – the 'Tivelah' – in the Bay instead of having to travel to Maryland for the immersion in the regular mikveh – the one we talked about before."

"Oh, good. I'm extremely grateful for that and in fact, for all you've done, Stephen. So what happens next?"

"Even though you were circumcised as an infant, we will still need to have a 'symbolic' circumcision, the 'hatafat dam brit,' which is merely exacting a drop of blood from the penis. I saw that wince! Sounds worse than it is, really. Just a pin dot of blood. Hurts for a second. I assure you, it's nothing worse than a novocaine needle you get at the dentist."

"Where will this 'hatafat dam brit' take place?"

"My suggestion is to have it done in the study of the Hillel House and the mohel has agreed."

"Tell me about a mohel again?"

"A mohel is a pious Jew who is given medical training sufficient to allow him to perform circumcisions."

"Could I have a urologist do it if I chose to?"

"We could do it that way, Matt, if I was present to say the Blessing."

"Well, I'm inclined to go along with tradition, as of this moment."

"Fine. I'll make the necessary arrangement."

"It's such a minimal procedure that we could go directly to the immersion. You know, Matt, the Baptists understood this in the context of Christianity. It is a transitional ritual – the rite of initiation into Judaism – not a matter of purification. You realized that, didn't you?"

"Yes. I've attended a couple of these and I remember the Rabbi's explanation."

"In a week or two, when you've completed your reading and we've had a chance to discuss what you've read, you'll take the written exam which the 'bet din' – the council – prepares. And there are some oral questions, as well. I have no doubt you'll sail through it," reassured Stephen.

"I'm not worried. Then?"

"Then after the 'hatafat dam brit,' the symbolic circumcision and the Tivelah – the immersion – the last step is for you to take your oath as a Jew and receive your

Hebrew name before the ark where the Torah scrolls are housed. There will be witnesses, chosen by the rabbinical council, and a prayer of acceptance you'll recite – that's about it."

"Oh, so we'll end up at The Hillel House then? Will you be acting as the Rabbi and make the pronouncements?"

"I will, unless the Rabbi comes in from Salisbury. We're not sure yet."

"Bess is talking about having wine and cakes and some kind of spread afterwards; kind of like a Briss!" Matthew smiled, thinking back to their discussion ('my baby boy becomes a Jew! How lovely' she had said, as she cradled his head in her lap, smothering him with kisses).

"You know, we Jews, Matt, we can't have an event without food and wine – from Birth to Bar Mitzvah, to Weddings – and even at Death!"

Stephen was suddenly aware of having used the word that he knew Matthew couldn't handle just yet. He came 'round to the front of his desk. For the first time in all the years he had known Matthew Held, he put his arm around his shoulders.

"Come on, I'll walk you to the car. Let's talk about this party Bess is planning. Hey, it's your coming-out, Matthew. Quite an event!"

"I'm probably the oldest convert in captivity, Stephen!"

"Oh, I doubt that! Will the party be at Carlisle Way or at Hillel?"

"I think Bess would prefer Carlisle Way!"

"No better place, Matt, for a party – for anything, right?"

"Yes, I've always believed so."

Matthew thought back to all the years of family

dinners and parties he and Bess prepared; Jewish holiday dinners, parties honoring a friend's birthday or a new grandchild. Even now, with her frailty, she wouldn't let him help her in the kitchen. Maggie came more often. But she let him do the floral arrangements and select the music.

The thought of living in Carlisle Way without Bess washed over him. He felt sickened within his stomach. Beads of perspiration began to form upon his forehead. On the way home, he drove slowly, picturing his bride the way she greeted him sixteen years ago – the lovely Bess Cantin, resplendent in beige chantilly lace, carrying roses of every color from the gardens of Carlisle Way.

MARGARET "MAGGIE" WILLIAMS was the last of her kind. She'd been tending to white southern ladies and their homes "nigh on to sixty years," she liked to say. When first they met, Bess, the young bride, was known in town as that "import from up north" and "a Jewess" besides!

After they got to know one another – when they actually became friends – Maggie and Bess would talk about the isolation that both Jews and blacks experienced in the southern community in which they found themselves.

It was 1956. Loudonville, Virginia, on the Eastern Shore, was reeling from the newly passed integration laws. White Supremacist groups were still meeting in secret to try to find a way to circumvent *Brown v. Board of Education*, decided by a unanimous U.S. Supreme Court.

"They don't cotton to no Jews neither, especially the Jews from up north." That's what Maggie told Bess not long after coming to work at Carlisle Way.

"Blacks and Jews – we'z cut from the same cloth,"

127

Maggie asserted. "Why, some of them Jewish boys – they done died for us – when we wuz marchin' in Selma and Birmingham! Blacks and Jews was marchin' and workin' together when we was havin' them freedom rides during the fifties. And it was them there young Jewish lawyers, along with our menfolks, who took our cases up to those big-city high courts and all. Some did it for nothin' – no money even! I hear 'bout all of this. Your peoples' still doin' stuff like that!" Margaret "Maggie" Williams was also the haute-dame philosopher of her ladies' church group, besides knowing just about everyone in town that mattered. She made Bess aware of those in Loudonville who harbored the most prejudice. "If they done hate blacks, they hate Jews, too!" She was usually right.

"You peoples made it 'cuz you done know the importance of learnin'. You Jewish mamas, and the menfolks too, but mostly it's them mamas, have been pushing them young'uns for as long as I knows. We needs to get these black children in college; finish high school at least, get a trade! 'Course, you havin' white skin and all didn't hurt you none!" And she and Bess would laugh 'til their sides hurt.

Surely Bess Cantin learned a lot about life in the south through the experienced eye of Margaret "Maggie" Williams. And the strong Jewish heritage that Bess brought with her from the north became a conduit through Maggie, some of which found its way into one small southern black Baptist church.

"Jew and blacks – we luv food, we luvs children, and we luvs dancin' and singin'! Them kugels and briskets – that chopped liver and matza balls – why, if that ain't soul food, then I don't know what soul food is!"

STEPHEN SMILED to himself remembering the

"Maggie" stories Bess was so fond of telling.

Maggie was the first housekeeper Bess Cantin ever hired, and she kept Maggie on for many years. At seventy-two, Maggie retired, except for nursing Bess this last year.

It wasn't long before Bess discovered that Maggie had "magic" hands, as she called them.

"By the time those young-uns of Ms. Cantin's was goin' off to college, she took me – sat me down – and 'splained to me she wanted I should learn 'bout some kind of nursin.' You didn't argue with Miss Bess, then, as now, 'cuz she was usually right. I means, 'bout most things... so I went. She 'n Dr. Dave, they paid for it, too, and I'd get off early so's she could drive me to the hospital. She didn't want me late for them classes."

She must have told Stephen Sohlberg this story a half-dozen times or so, but he didn't mind hearing it again right now. Maggie knew how much stock Dr. Steve placed in Bess Cantin and how he needed some cheering-up, what with that cancer eating her up and all.

"When I first started working for Miss Bess and Dr. Dave, she didn't know no different 'bout conversin' with coloreds – I means blacks. She'd talk with me like I was one of her white lady friends! If she was at home and it was lunchtime, she'd fix me a sandwich. Make me sit right down with her! We'd be yakkin' 'bout raisin up children or 'bout you menfolks; all your strange ways, us smilin' at each other behind Dr. Dave's back and all. Sometimes we even talked about you, Dr. Steve! And when she saw I'd be waitin' on Luke, my husband, God rest his soul, to fetch me to work and pick me up, she saz, 'Now Maggie, isn't it time you entered the twentieth century? I'm going to teach you to drive!' And teach me she did, and she and Dr. Dave got me a little second-hand car, and me tootin' 'round town as big as life!

129

"Why, Miss Bess'd have me drivin' 'round the neighborhood, teachin' me and all – and in the driveway – backin' up and going forwards – what with them ladies peeping out at us from behind their curtains! I tell you, we raised some eyebrows 'round here – 'round Carlisle Way. When my Luke taught little Alex how to play kickball right in front of this-here fancy house – why, white childrens came a-runnin' from all over the neighborhood to join in!"

So when Stephen Sohlberg came to see Bess this day, the day of Alex and Jan's wedding, all done up in his special wedding-guest clothes, Maggie stood to leave Bess' bedside.

"Don't be tiring her out none, Dr. Steve, what with all them 'shrink' stories you always tellin' 'bout!"

"Don't you worry your sweet old head, Maggie! Why don't you go downstairs and be a part of the celebration? Of course, you never did like Alex much!"

Maggie smiled. "That boy! Been a man since he was up to my knees and in britches! I knows he'd make a fine doctor, too, just like Dr. Dave! I'll go and sit toward the back – case you needs me."

Bess wanted to tell her to sit up front with the family. But knowing Maggie, she knew she wouldn't hear of it. So she just let it go. Bess had had to let a lot of things go lately.

Patting the bed, Bess motioned for Stephen to come and sit close by her side.

"Whenever the pain becomes too much, I bring you 'online' Stephen. It's a recurring dream about you and me. I've been having it ever since we...."

"Don't talk now, Bess. Please, get some rest."

"Not right now, Stephen. I've always wanted to share this dream with you, but I never could recall all of it. Now it's crystal clear!"

Stephen held Bess' hand, squeezing it gently.

"All right, Bess, I'm listening."

"I close my eyes and you and I, Stephen, we are dancing the wedding dance under a chupah – in an old Russian shtetl in the late 1880's. The village women are saying, 'That Rivkalah – my name in the dream – she's so much older than our young Rabbi, and such a plain one, not pretty like her sister.' You see darling, because you *are* a Jewish scholar, and a 'tzadech,' a man of knowledge, you became a Rabbi in my dream!"

As she spoke, a soft smile enveloped Bess' face.

"You had married my sister Sara. But she died in childbirth and you had no one to care for your new baby boy. You and I had hardly ever spoken two words to each other! If I wasn't helping my mother in the kitchen or my father with the animals, I would sneak off in the corner to read. The villagers all said I was too 'bookish' and too stuck on myself to ever find a husband.

"Even the matchmakers gave up on me! I was a spinster at the age of twenty-five, considered old in those days.

"But you came to my father and asked for my hand in marriage. 'It is not an arranged marriage,' said my mother. 'She is needed here to help with the chores – the milking, the crops,' spoke my father, 'and she has no dowry – only a small collection of books, which are worthless to a woman!'

"But Ephraim – that is your name in the dream! – had observed me during his courtship with Sara and during their brief marriage. 'She will make a fine rebetzin,' – a rabbi's wife – you told my father. And then the dream begins to fade and all I see is your smiling face, and you're dancing with me under the chupah! We take hold of the kerchief and dance and dance in a circle, our bodies barely touching, as we balefully eye one another and my heart is pounding, for I had secretly loved you, even when Sara was betrothed to you!"

Stephen's throat tightened – went dry. He placed one arm behind her and with his other, he supported her back and pulled her up carefully from the bed pillows.

Kissing her softly, he held her as gently as he could. He wanted to hold her tightly; hold on to her forever, but she was so breakable all of a sudden. He tried to let her down easily, but she wouldn't put her head back down on the pillows.

"Stephen, help me up, please. I want to see some of the wedding from my balcony!"

Stephen tried to talk her out of it, explaining about the coolness of the late September air. But she would hear none of it. And so he obliged Bess by helping her on with her woolen robe.

"If you sit on the side of the bed, Bess, I'll put on your slippers."

"Oh, my sweet Stephen" she said while patting his head, "I'll even wear my shawl, over there on the chair, just to please you!"

As he knelt before her, placing the slippers on her thin, white feet, she leaned over and kissed his bald spot. "There," she said, "I've always wanted to do that!" Still on his knees, Stephen put his head in Bess' lap, choking back his tears. She lifted his chin and she bent down to kiss him. He could no longer hold back. He had done so for too many years. He kissed her cheeks, then her mouth. "Bess, oh my Bess. How I've loved you!"

"I know, Stephen. I've always known. My heart was full because of you. Now come with me. Let's share this moment – Alex and Jan's moment!"

Bess had had wheels placed on her favorite bedroom chaise. When she was ready for the outdoors, Stephen pushed the chaise onto the outdoor porch which Bess referred to as "her balcony."

Down below the guests were milling about, many of whom were being ushered into their seats. The ceremony was to begin momentarily.

Rows of chairs were set at angles; then fanned out within Carlisle Way's rear gardens. Bathed in white calla lillies and set within reams of white satin ribbon and bows, Carlisle Way had never looked more elegant. Touches of Bess Cantin were everywhere. She and Jan had planned the decorations and music long before Bess' illness had taken hold. Green ferns, taken from its abundant roots at Carlisle Way, were wound around and covered the chupah's four white poles and then lain in sheaths across its top, yet still allowing room for sun and sky to bask upon the young lovers.

Matthew had rigged up an intricate electronic audio system so that those in the rear could hear the ceremony. But mostly it was for Bess' ears, as Matthew knew she would not be joining the others. Harp, viola and piano alternated selections of baroque music, lending an atmosphere of yesteryear.

To carry out the theme of Sukkot, Bess' favorite holiday, and one which Alex himself had greatly enjoyed as a child when visiting Carlisle Way, Matthew had ordered a large white tent with a secret flap over the chupah which was now opened on this clear day, but could also be ready to shield those under the chupah if rain were to appear. Vines that were in blossom hung everywhere, giving forth fragrance, along with the traditional fruits of Sukkot.

Matt looked up, waved, and threw a kiss to Bess. She returned it by kissing her finger first and then blowing him a kiss as if it were a cigarette of smoke. Matt motioned to Stephen to hurry, by way of pointing to his watch. Stephen leaned over the porch railing and called Matthew to come closer so he could tell him something.

"I'm going to stay here with Bess 'til the ceremony's over. Okay? Then you come up and relieve me!"

Matt nodded in agreement. He began walking toward the guests. But something stopped him. Abruptly, he walked back to just below the balcony and gazed up at Bess and Stephen.

Cupping his mouth with his hands and calling up toward them, he smiled, while admonishing Stephen to take care of "his girl."

Bess reached for Stephen's hand. Together they watched Jan and Alex as they stood under the chupah, listening to the words of the wedding liturgy.

"May He who is supreme in power, blessing and glory, bless this bridegroom and this bride. May He who helps us see the sacred dimension of all life, guide this bridegroom and bride to the realization of sanctity and devotion every day as today. Help them to renew their love continually, as you renew creation. May their concern for each other reflect Your concern for all men; may their loving faithfulness reflect Your love. Throughout the years, may they hallow their life together, that the home they establish become a blessing to all Israel. May Your light illuminate their lives. And let us say: Amen."

Bess and Stephen uttered the "Amen," as well.

"In happiness and joy, we thank God for His blessing of love, which we celebrate today, formally consecrating the love of Janet Faith Cohen and Alex Charles Goodman for each other.

"May they always rejoice in their love, graced by

delight through their mutual affection. O Lord, our God, Source of all blessing, fulfill every worthy wish of their hearts. Open their eyes to the beauty and the mystery of the love they hold for each other, every day as today. May their life together embrace and nurture the promise of this moment, so that all who know them will call them truly blessed. And let us say: Amen.

"Enjoy life with the woman you love," the Rabbi continued, looking squarely now at Alex, "all the days of your life which He has given you under the sun, for that is your portion in life and in your toil at which you toil under the sun. Whatever your hand finds to do, do it with your might!"

Bess tightened her grip on Stephen's hand. "Whatever your hand finds to do, do it with your might," she said, repeating the words she had just heard and knowing full well the Rabbi chose this part of the wedding text because of Alex's well-known desire to become a surgeon.

The Rabbi was now holding the full cup of wine as he recited the wine blessing. First the wine is presented to the bridegroom and then to the bride. The Rabbi spoke: "As you share the wine of this cup, so may you share *all* things from this day on with love and with understanding."

It was Jan's turn to speak, as she turned and faced Alex. "My beloved speaks and says to me: 'Arise, my love, my fair one, and come away. For lo, the winter is past, the rain is over and gone. The flowers appear on the earth; the time of singing has come, and the voice of the turtledove is heard in our land. The fig tree puts forth its figs and the vines are in blossom; they give forth fragrance!"

Alex, gazing lovingly at Jan, answered with these words: "Arise, my love, my fair one, and come away. Oh, my dove, in the clefts of the rock, in the covert of the cliff, let me see your face, let me hear your voice, for your voice is sweet and your face is lovely."

Bess smiled. Stephen recalled the prayer's significance; this promise which speaks to the heart of hope and renewal.

Before the breaking of the glass, the Rabbi added the blessing, "May the Lord bless you and keep you. May He cause His countenance to shine upon you and be gracious unto you. May the Lord lift up His countenance upon you and grant you peace."

AS STEPHEN looked on, he noted for the first time the way Jan held herself. Her hair, the way she wore it, the elongated curve of her back – that carriage. It was as if he was witnessing Bess Friedman on the day of her wedding to David Cantin.

If he had made known his feelings toward Bess years ago, would it have mattered? Before Sylvia? Before David? Back then, at the University, in undergraduate school, he knew Bess cared for him. But he could never adequately gauge whether it was admiration, friendship or something more.

While Bess was ebullient, Sylvia was mercurial. Where Bess never seemed to need anyone, Sylvia was wholly dependent upon him, even then. Sylvia's was a dark and brooding beauty whereas Bess' was golden and spontaneous. Perhaps it was Sylvia's self-effacing manner that aroused him to be her protector. But what had once attracted him to Sylvia had become his nemesis. Gradually, over the years, her neuroses had developed. What had been charming eccentricity had become a yoke – it required an effort to endure. Yet his allegiance to Sylvia and the boys was steadfast.

No utterance of his love for Bess fell from his lips, until she came to him and reopened the wound. By then David was ill and she needed his help. After David had passed away, Stephen wanted to be more than Bess' "spiritual" lover. He wanted them to spend the rest of their lives together. But then, Sylvia was ailing. Devotion, honor, all the precepts he had based his life on were at stake. Enter Matthew Held. In all of his self-inflicted musings and inner debate, he had not counted on there being another man in Bess Cantin's life other than himself.

Stephen's thoughts had wandered as they were prone to do of late. The four of them – David and Bess, he and Sylvia – were neighbors and friends all through med school and in the early years of establishing their families and practices here in Loudonville. In the latter years of undergraduate school, Bess fell in love with David. Handsome, articulate, suave even then, and from one of the wealthiest and most prestigious families in Loudonville, David Cantin could have had any woman on campus. He only wanted Bess Friedman, and he got her without a challenger in sight! Stephen Sohlberg, never the competitor, afraid of rejection, remained silent.

As Jan turned to face Alex, as she declared her marital vows, the profile was Bess'! The lovely shape of the head tilted toward her shoulder. Supplicating, yet confident, just as Bess was at that same stage of life. Was Alex aware of their likeness? Stephen had never noticed until now. As he maneuvered his chair around so he could share his discovery with Bess, he saw her eyes were tilted downward – her hand, cold and limp within his own.

"Bess? Oh, pray God! Bess, love of my life! How will I live without seeing your smile? I will miss you so! I'll keep my eye on Matthew for you. I know you wanted to ask me this, but didn't – couldn't. I'll keep him close, for you, Bess!"

So as not to shift attention to the balcony where he and Bess had been viewing the ceremony, Stephen waited until Alex had stomped and crushed the covered glass. As the guests applauded the newlyweds, Stephen wheeled the chaise back into the bedroom.

Sensing something amiss – perhaps the only one in the crowd who did – Matthew peered upward toward Bess' room. He caught sight of Stephen's back as he was wheeling Bess into the bedroom. Matthew quietly withdrew into the crowd, making his way up the back steps.

Stephen had lifted Bess onto the bed, smoothing the covers around her, tucking them in, as one might do for a child – or a loved one. The light that had sifted through the slatted blinds cast its shadow in a way that gave Bess' skin a luminous quality.

Stephen sat squarely on the bed now, knowing full well, even before he placed his head upon her chest, that he would not find even a trace of a heartbeat. He had barely to touch her eyelids and they closed.

Matthew opened the bedroom door. He knew it was over. She wouldn't have to bear the pain any longer. There was that to be thankful for.

"Stephen – come, Stephen – we have to let her go now," Matthew said hesitantly as he gently touched Stephen's arm. Stephen stood slowly, as if in a trance. "I'll leave you alone with her, Matt, if you like."

"No, Stephen, please, please stay. I want to know her last words before she let go, before she...." He simply could not say "died." Someday, perhaps. But not yet.

"She said, 'tell Matthew he was my other self. However much he loved me, I loved him more.'"

Matthew and Stephen embraced as brothers.

"Matt, let's not tell Alex and Jan, or any of the family just yet – maybe not 'til the reception is over. All right with you?"

Matthew nodded in agreement.

"After the funeral, after the thirty days of mourning, Stephen, I want to keep her memory alive. You and I. We loved her – we can – I mean, we can go to the cemetery, talk to her. And other days, we can talk to each other about her – things she loved to do, words she used, expressions – you know what I'm talking about. Will you help me, Stephen? Can you do that?"

"Yes, Matt. I can do what you've asked."

Matthew was thinking aloud. "I want to say 'The Kaddish'– the prayer in memory of a loved one. Isn't that what it's called? Before, it was just a word – a prayer you told me to study for my conversion. But we don't have the ten people required by Jewish law to pray with – the 'minyan,' I think you say. But I want to say a prayer *now* – right here. With just you and Bess – just the three of us. Can we?"

Holding Matthew by the shoulders as if to steady him, but in truth, to fortify himself, Stephen replied, "Yes, of course, I'll get a prayer book from Bess' study.

"Stay here, Matt. Maggie can sit by the door. I'll get her. I'll explain. She won't let Alex or anyone in until we've had our prayer. Then we must see to the family."

Stephen returned with the Weekday Prayer Book in hand. "Matt, before we recite this prayer – I've chosen the Psalm of David – we must say the traditional brukah or prayer, you know... the one upon hearing bad news." Stephen reached into his pocket for his skullcap. Matthew was still wearing his from the wedding ceremony.

Reaching for Bess' manicuring scissors which lay upon her dressing table, Stephen made a small tear on

Matthew's jacket lapel and then another on his own shirt, the pocket which lay closest to the heart. Matthew recalled the tradition. It was a symbol – the tearing or wrenching away from the heart.

In a halting voice, he led Matthew to say, "Barukh attah adonai eloheinu melekh ho-alam, dayan ha-emet. Praised are You, Lord our God, King of the Universe, the true Judge."

So far, before even the mourning process had begun, Matthew knew that the vocabulary of his newfound religion would give meaning to his sorrow. He reminded himself of the last meeting with Stephen when they had discussed the prospect of Bess' death. Stephen had said, "The finest part of a human being is not subject to decay, Matt. The power of ideas; beauty, truth, ideals, values, all of these are home to the soul." And he, Matthew, would see that her soul would survive – her values embraced.

They prayed together aloud:

The earth is the Lord's and its fullness;
All the world; all its inhabitants.
He founded it upon the seas;
He set it firm upon flowing waters.

Who may ascend the mountain of the Lord?
Who may stand in His holy place?
He who has clean hands and a pure heart,
He who takes not His name in vain, swearing falsely.

He will receive a blessing from the Lord,
a just reward from the God of his deliverance.
Such is the generation of those who seek Him,
who, like Jacob, long for His Presence.

BOTH MEN now positioned themselves so that they stood on each side of the bed. After the prayer had been completed, they carefully drew the covers over Bess' face, as was the custom.

Matthew said aloud, as if no one else was present. "Yes, the Psalm of David was a most fitting prayer. The purest of hearts was my beloved Bess' and if anyone should ascend the mountain of the Lord, it will be she. You chose well, Stephen. I believe Bess would have liked those words."

"I think so, too, Matt. Shall we go? It's time. The others will need us now."

The Lord gave, and the Lord has taken away.
Blessed be the name of the Lord for the years
in-between the giving and the taking away.

A Rabbinical scholar's interpretation from Job

I place my soul in God's palm, whether awake or asleep.
My body is with God, my soul too, and
since God is with me, I have no fear.

Last two lines of "Adon Olom" Hebrew Prayerbook

Love is strong as death; many waters cannot extinguish love.

Song of Songs 8:6-7

The Lord's angel is on guard around those who revere Him,
and rescues them.
… and see how good is the Lord; blessed be the one who takes
refuge in Him.

The Hebrew Bereavement Service

BIBLIOGRAPHY AND FURTHER READING

The National Holocaust Museum, Washington, D.C.

The Simon Wiesenthal Center, Los Angeles, CA

The Hebrew Immigrant Society (HIAS), New York, NY.

The Unwanted, by Michael Marrus

DPs: Europe's Displaced Persons, 1945–1951, Mark Wyman

When Bad Things Happen to Good People, by Harold Kushner

Torah Today: A Renewed Encounter with Scripture, by Pinchas H. Peli

CPSIA information can be obtained at www.ICGtesting.com

260457BV00001B/2/P

9 780984 333967